Brad Stam
(617) 498-3907

English
National
Opera
Guide

7

Otello

Verdi

English National Opera
receives financial
assistance from the Arts
Council of Great Britain
and the Greater London
Council.

Ramon Vinay as the Moor and Otakar Kraus as Iago in the Covent Garden production of 1955, conducted by Kubelik. (Covent Garden Archives)

Preface

English National Opera Guides are companions to opera in performance. They contain articles and illustrations relevant to any production as well as those mounted by English National Opera. Of interest to all opera-lovers, also, is the complete original libretto, side by side with an English translation. There are many reasons why sung words may not be clearly distinguishable, whatever the language and however excellent the performance. The composer may have set several lines of text together, for instance, or he may have demanded an orchestral sound through which no voice could clearly articulate. ENO Guides give English readers the opportunity to know a libretto in advance and so greatly increase their understanding and enjoyment of performances whether live, broadcast or recorded.

ENO is very grateful to Barclays Bank for sponsoring this *Otello* Guide, as well as a new production, in its wide-ranging programme of community service. Such sponsorship is an indication of a steadily growing public interest in opera, and we hope the Guides will prove useful to new and experienced opera-lovers alike. An audience which knows what to look and listen for — one that demands a high standard of performance and recognises it when it is achieved — is our best support and, of course, an assurance for the future of opera in the English-speaking world.

Nicholas John
Editor

7

Otello

Giuseppe Verdi

English National Opera Guides Series Editor:
Nicholas John

This Guide is sponsored by **BARCLAYS BANK**

John Calder ● London
Riverrun Press ● New York

First published in Great Britain, 1981, by
John Calder (Publishers) Ltd.,
18 Brewer Street, London W1R 4AS

and

First published in the U.S.A., 1981, by
Riverrun Press Inc.,
175 Fifth Avenue,
New York, NY10010

BRITISH LIBRARY CATALOGUING IN PUBLICATION DATA

Otello. — (English National Opera Guides; 7)
    1. Verdi, Giuseppe. Otello
    2. Operas – Librettos
    I. Verdi, Giuseppe   II. John, Nicholas
    III. Boito, Arrigo   IV. Series
    782.1'092'4   ML410.V4

ISBN 0 – 7145 – 3850 – 7

Typeset in Plantin by Margaret Spooner Typesetting
Printed by The Hunter Rose Company Ltd., Toronto, Canada

Contents

List of Illustrations

Otello: The Background

Winton Dean

Verdi's career, like Wagner's, covered a vast span, not only in years but in artistic development. While every great artist matures with experience, expanding his expressive range and technical control, few have moved further from their starting point than the two giants of nineteenth-century opera. It is some measure of their creative vitality and powers of self-criticism that the hands that penned the crudities of *Nabucco* and *Rienzi* became capable of the utmost refinement in *Otello* and *Falstaff*, *The Ring* and *Parsifal*. From an almost regressive stance in youth they reached a position well in advance not only of their own generation but of the next, and they moulded the future course of opera. Yet we owe it to a near-miracle that Verdi's two last and greatest operas were ever written.

Ostensibly Verdi retired from the theatre with the production of *Aida* in 1871. Apart from the Requiem and the revised versions of *Simon Boccanegra* and *Don Carlos* he was silent for sixteen years, though the last three were occupied with the composition of *Otello*. He grew increasingly surly in his attitude to the world, grimly accepting what he chose to regard as his dismissal as a back-number. Two factors played a part in his return to the fold. One was his lifelong preoccupation with Shakespeare, the dramatist he admired above all others and whom, unlike the authors of his own Romantic generation, he never outgrew. His only Shakespeare opera so far had been *Macbeth*, produced in 1847 and revised for Paris in 1865. It was his favourite among his early works, and he planned to follow it with a *King Lear*. He reverted constantly to this project, and set more than one librettist to work on it. Cammarano produced a draft in 1850, Somma a complete libretto, after two years of correspondence, in 1855. It was considered before and after *A Masked Ball*, (1859, the Fool, like Oscar, was to be a *travesti* part), and Boito did some work on it even after *Falstaff* (1893). Verdi abandoned the idea reluctantly (he complained of the difficulty of finding suitable singers); if any of the music was composed, he destroyed it, though the words of one of Cordelia's arias found their way into Act One of *The Force of Destiny*. But he could not get Shakespeare out of his system.

The second factor was his relationship with Arrigo Boito, an ambitious composer as well as a poet, and a man not only of wide culture but of supreme intelligence and tact, whose admiration for Verdi knew no bounds. His opera *Mefistofele*, a failure in 1868 but very successful after extensive revision in 1875, is a work with an individual flavour that still repays occasional revival. Boito too was an admirer of Shakespeare. In 1862, at the age of twenty, he wrote a remarkably fine libretto on *Hamlet*, set by Franco Faccio (better remembered as conductor than composer) and produced in 1865; one can only regret that it did not fall into the hands of Verdi, who later expressed a high opinion of it. But Verdi's relations with Boito ran an eccentric course. They had collaborated as early as 1862 on the *Hymn of the Nations*, commissioned for the London Exhibition of that year. Boito and Faccio, close friends and a full generation younger than Verdi, belonged to a clamorous avant-garde group given to airing iconoclastic opinions about their seniors. In November 1863, on the production of an opera by Faccio, Boito recited and published an ode looking forward to the restoration of pure Italian art 'on the

Francesco Tamagno as Otello.   *Martinelli, at Covent Garden.*

altar now defiled like the wall of a brothel'. Verdi, always touchy in his pride, took this as a personal insult and often quoted it sarcastically (and inaccurately) in his letters over the next sixteen years. Without the dogged efforts of Giulio Ricordi, son of the publisher, to bring about a fruitful reconciliation, regardless of snubs from the composer, *Otello* and *Falstaff* could never have come to birth.

For the better part of two decades Ricordi played Verdi with the patience of an angler confronted by a particularly wily old salmon. When Verdi did take the fly, it was no easy matter to bring him to the bank, and more than once he nearly got off the hook. About the time of *Aida* (1871) Ricordi tried to interest him in the libretto of *Nerone*, the opera on which Boito laboured for more than half his life and still left unfinished. Ricordi even persuaded Boito to renounce the libretto in Verdi's favour, an astonishing act of abnegation on the part of a man whose hopes were centred on this work. Verdi refused to bite. In November 1871 he and Boito had a chance encounter in Bologna station at 3 a.m. after a performance of *Lohengrin*; they discussed nothing of moment and did not meet again for nearly eight years. At this period Verdi was bitter about the influence of Wagner on the younger Italians, and in particular about the charge of imitating Wagner brought against himself; his snide references to Boito's 1863 ode show that he had not forgiven its author.

Ricordi's plan began at last to germinate in the summer of 1879, when Verdi, without committing himself in any way, encouraged Boito to start work on the libretto of *Otello*. He was still very wary; on receiving the first version in November he placed it (ominously) beside Somma's *Re Lear* and did not begin to set it for nearly five more years. However the collaboration was launched in the winter of 1880-81 with the revision of *Simon Boccanegra*. Whether or not Verdi intended this as a trial run, he was justifiably pleased with the result and with Boito's work. The 1881 *Boccanegra* is a masterpiece – not flawless (that could hardly be expected from the revision of a work nearly 25 years old), but a striking transformation of the patchy opera of 1857, whose bold sallies into the future contrast painfully with descents into the crudity of Verdi's earliest period. The magnificent new Act One finale in the council chamber is much closer to the style of *Otello* than anything Verdi had yet written; and both poet and composer invested the villain Paolo with many traits we now recognise in the portrait of Iago.

A principal reason for the unevenness of Verdi's middle-period operas, those that followed *La Traviata*, lay in the blood-and-thunder romanticism of the literary sources, a vein Verdi was rapidly outgrowing. The Spanish plays dating from the 1830s, on which the 1857 *Boccanegra, The Force of Destiny* and the earlier *Il Trovatore* were based, concentrated on a multiplicity of incident at the expense of character. They depended so much on coincidence as to impede Verdi's deepening insight into the subtleties of human motivation, an insight that might be called Shakespearean. *Les Vêpres Siciliennes (The Sicilian Vespers)* nearly collapses under the creaking mechanism of Scribe's old-fashioned plot, and *A Masked Ball* is saved from the same fate only by the introduction of a comic element, a strain of Gallic mockery, which lightens the texture and steers the melodramatic story clear of bathos. Significantly this was the only middle-period opera that Verdi did not substantially revise. In the next opera, *The Force of Destiny* he endeavoured to combine comedy, tragedy and romantic adventure on a larger scale, possibly with Shakespeare's history plays at the back of his mind. The result is fascinating but incoherent. The long arm of coincidence becomes extended like an elephant's trunk; the plot suggests the operation not so much of destiny as of far-fetched contrivance, and for all its glorious music the attempt to evoke a multifarious world of serious and comic characters carries only fitful conviction. The next three operas, *Don Carlos, Aida* and *Otello*, contain no comic characters or situations; their ironies are tragic and bitter. Only in *Falstaff* did Verdi succeed in striking a balance of extremes, and then by approaching from the opposite direction: Ford's jealousy, as potentially dangerous as Otello's, fits into the over-all conception as the comic characters of *Forza* do not.

Don Carlos is the most ambitious of these intermediate operas, and the most successful, thanks in part to the stature of Schiller's drama. The intertwined themes of personal and political destiny against a huge historical canvas presented the most arduous challenge Verdi ever set himself. The danger here was one of scale. The first version as composed and rehearsed (it was heavily cut before performance in 1867), and even as given in Paris, is so enormously long as to strain the comfort and attention of a normal audience. Verdi could not adopt Wagner's expedient (unwillingly accepted by Berlioz in another mighty conception, *The Trojans*) of splitting it into more than one evening. When he revised and shortened the opera for Italy in 1884 he made many improvements, but gravely impaired his design by lopping off the first act. He left a torso; fortunately we can make amends by restoring the Fontainebleau act and combining it with the changes and contractions of 1884.

In *Aida*, and even more in *Otello*, Verdi judged the proportions exactly. Shakespeare's world in *Othello*, though less all-embracing than Schiller's in *Don Carlos*, is sufficiently complex to have daunted any ordinary librettist. Rossini's *Otello* of 1816, then still in the repertory and regarded as an Italian classic, is a by no means unworthy specimen of Romantic *opera seria*; but for two of the three acts the librettist made mincemeat of Shakespeare. Iago, not married to Emilia (who becomes a colourless confidante), is a rejected suitor of Desdemona; the handkerchief is replaced by an intercepted and insufficiently addressed letter; there is no Cassio, but a great deal of Desdemona's heavy father. For two acts Otello is little more than a touchy tenor with an ungovernable temper; he has no love music, and no scene with Desdemona before the murder. All this would not be worth recalling except for two facts. In the last act Rossini and his librettist reverted unexpectedly to Shakespeare, including the tragic end, very rare at that period (though Rossini was misguided enough to change it later); and rising as if by instinct to the challenge, they created one of the finest scenes in Italian Romantic opera. Secondly, Rossini's treatment of the Willow Song and especially of Desdemona's prayer, an addition to Shakespeare, was not lost on Verdi.

Rossini's opera has one Shakespearean act; Verdi's is true to the spirit of the play throughout, though there are inevitable omissions and some of the characters, notably Iago, are modified. Boito's compression of the story – or rather his reconstruction of it in operatic terms – is masterly. Where Rossini's characters never leave Venice, Verdi's never appear there: the opera begins with the Moor's arrival in Cyprus. This involved the amputation of Shakespeare's first act. But Boito's surgery was far more skilful than that to which *Don Carlos* was subjected. He contrived to incorporate into the remaining acts not only the essential information on which the plot is founded but some of the dialogue as well. He ran a major risk in taking as read the key event of Desdemona's marriage in defiance of her father (which occupied Rossini for two acts); yet he turned this to positive advantage by his treatment of the Act One love duet, a most original conception. Passionate love duets between husband and wife are very rare in opera, and virtually unknown early in the action when the machinery of the plot has barely been set in motion. In *Otello* this placing becomes the fulcrum of the whole opera; it establishes in depth the beauty of the relationship which the machinations of evil are to destroy.

Verdi by this date was capable of expressing in music almost any subtlety of human character; one might say that he had outrun every literary model except Shakespeare. He had so refined his style that he could convey the most elusive innuendo, whether in the vocal line or the orchestra. But whereas Wagner's endless melody differed radically from the square rhythms and heavy tread of his early operas—a revolution obvious to the whole musical world, which acclaimed or denounced it with equal frenzy—Verdi worked outwards from within. For that reason his quieter revolution received less acclaim. Although he had left the *cabaletta* and the reiterated accompaniment figure far behind, he never, even in *Falstaff*, abandoned the set number. The very fact that he retained it, while softening its edges through the infinitely flexible *arioso* that had superceded regular recitative, gave his last operas an extra tensile strength. *Otello* is full of pieces that conform in general outline to the traditional plan of Italian opera—the storm and bonfire choruses, Iago's *brindisi* and Credo, the love duet, the choral serenade in Act Two, the handkerchief quartet, the male trio and finale of Act Three, Desdemona's Willow Song and *Ave Maria*—but they are handled with such dexterity that we seldom think of their conventional forbears. There is no creaking at the joints, and no surplus tissue. The pacing of the opera, the balance between musical form and the progress of the action, attains a perfection that has perhaps never been surpassed. Every episode works on several simultaneous interacting levels. Since the pace of music is so much slower than that of words, only such a complex economy could have realised within reasonable limits a drama which, while different from Shakespeare's in emphasis, falls nowhere below it as a work of art.

Romilda Pantaleoni as Desdemona. Although she created the role at La Scala, she did not please Verdi, and did not achieve a world fame like her colleagues Tamagno and Maurel. (Stuart-Liff Collection)

For all this Boito deserves to share the credit. *Othello* lends itself less easily than most Shakespeare plays—much less than *Macbeth*—to the aria-ensemble structure of an Italian nineteenth-century opera. Nearly all the movements mentioned above were devised by Boito, who had followed the same plan in adapting *Hamlet* for Faccio; some of them, such as the Credo and the serenade, have no exact counterpart in the play but enormously enhance the opera. With the finale of Act Three Boito did more. Verdi was dissatisfied with the first version, and in August 1880 proposed to end the act with an assault by the Turks, an offstage battle, and a curtain with Desdemona alone praying for Otello's victory. Boito silently made the change; only later, when pressed by Verdi, did he point out that this would disperse the accumulated tension and undermine the psychology of the last act.

When Verdi at length began to compose the music in March 1884, the whole project was at once brought to the verge of disaster by a blunder in the press. Boito was reported to have said in Naples that he had written the libretto unwillingly and now regretted his inability to set it himself. Verdi promptly offered to return it. Boito's tact, matched this time by Verdi's generosity, saved the situation, and work was resumed at the end of the year. After that there were no hitches, although Verdi was inactive throughout the summer of 1885. He finished the composition sketch in October, the scoring and some revision by the end of 1886. The first performance at La Scala, Milan, on February 5, 1887, was a triumph. It was conducted by Faccio, with whom Verdi had long been reconciled (an even greater conductor, Arturo Toscanini, played the cello in the orchestra); and the composer insisted that his "incomparable librettist" (Frank Walker's words) should share the applause.

Verdi and Boito at Sant' Agata. (Archivio Storico Ricordi)

'Otello': Drama and Music

Benedict Sarnaker

After some thirty years of hard work (he called it slavery) serving the conventions and audiences of Italian opera, Verdi retired. He was financially secure and preferred farming and philanthropy to the heart-breaking struggle of operatic production. How Verdi was cajoled by friends and his crafty publisher Giulio Ricordi into overcoming his distrust of Arrigo Boito; how they collaborated on *Otello* and *Falstaff* (as well as the revision of *Simon Boccanegra*); and how Boito became a close friend, then one of the few people whom Verdi trusted and finally a surrogate son who was at the composer's bedside when Verdi died, has been delicately chronicled by Frank Walker in *The Man Verdi*. Their operatic achievement has been richly praised and, in truth, *Otello* rivals Shakespeare in passion and tenderness. Moreover, where Shakespeare (in order to make Desdemona's pleas for Cassio seem more credible) is forced to spread his play, the opera, by using a contrast of musical styles, achieves a similar effect with more force and compression than its model.

The first act of Shakespeare's *Othello** is set in Venice and deals with the love of Desdemona for the Moorish general Othello. Their secret marriage infuriates her father; a court action follows and reveals that their love is true. The irate father is somewhat placated and Othello is ordered as Governor to Cyprus to defend the Venetian colony against the attacking Turks. Boito and Verdi abandon this act (thus shortening a very long play and allowing time for music), but keep its function: the establishment of the personality and relationship of the chief characters. The operatic first act is constructed of a string of traditional operatic numbers (storm, victory hymn, fireside chorus, drinking-song, love duet) but, less conventionally, these are closely linked both by action which continues during and between the numbers, and by an unbroken musical fabric.

There is no overture—not even a prelude. An horrific crash raises the curtain and explodes a raging storm upon the stage. The effect is chaotic: figures heard dashing to and fro in the dark and rain are thrown into visible relief by flashes of lightning, whilst thunder is punctuated by canon-shots signalling out to sea (all these scenic elements are precisely orchestrated by Verdi and meticulously positioned in the score). Otello's ship is briefly sighted. For a moment it seems that it will sink and the excited spectators counterpoint the fractured turmoil with a great hymn to heaven [1]: 'With gestures of horror and supplication, facing towards the sea-bastion', command the stage instructions. Nowhere in Italian opera had such a powerful and exactly orchestrated storm been heard. Storms there were in plenty. They were designed to suspend the action, to increase tension and give the orchestra a brief moment of glory (a splendid example can be found towards the end of Rossini's *The Barber of Seville*), but none broke so viciously nor were any driven so furiously—and none injected character and action so potently as this.

Just after the crowd's appeal for help we meet the first of the three

*For convenience *Othello* refers to Shakespeare's play, *Otello* to the opera. By analogy, references to the title role will be made thus: Othello (Shakespeare), Otello (Verdi).

protagonists—and Iago (baritone) instantly shows his malevolence: '*E infranto l'artimon!* ... *L'alvo frenetico del mar sia la sua tomba*' (lit.) 'Her mainsail's split in two ... May the raging belly of the sea be her tomb!' No sooner uttered than his evil wish is thwarted: 'She is safe now!' cry the Cypriots and a few moments later Otello (tenor) enters [2]. There is no more striking an entry for tenor in opera—nor a more difficult one, for Otello must run onto the stage and launch a ringing, heroic line (reaching high A) without even one word of recitative to help him. In only three lines of verse Otello unequivocally establishes his stature as a commander and leader—the Cypriots respond instantly with a joyous chorus '*Evviva Otello*'. Although Otello's opening words elicit such happiness in his subjects, his command that they should rejoice because the Turkish enemy is defeated will ring with deep irony as the work grows. The happy chorus ends and the storm subsides. As the chorus comment on this ('*Si calma la bufera*' 'A calm succeeds the storm now'—this too will echo ironically), we sense a wonderful relaxation of tension—Verdi achieves this by releasing a disturbingly discordant low pedal-point on three adjacent semitones $(C—C\#—D)$ which an organ had held from the very opening of the work.

In this easier atmosphere Iago turns to Roderigo (tenor), a simple-minded young Venetian hopelessly in love with Desdemona, and encourages his passion, assuring him that Desdemona will soon tire of her husband[3]. Iago also confesses that he hates Cassio for being promoted before him and that he hates Otello for making that promotion—and ends one of his unctuous phrases with the rolling trill which will mark many of his most characteristic utterances. The two move off upstage (and out of earshot) whilst the Cypriots light a bonfire and start to sing ('*Fuoco di gioia*', 'Flame of rejoicing') in praise of fire. This is another cliché of Italian opera, and Verdi himself described it (in a letter to Giulio Ricordi) as "that wretched bonfire scene". Despite this off-hand dismissal of the chorus, its swift, light scoring is a delight and its function in the act is essential since it forms an integral part of a carefully graded transition from the explosive opening to the serene final duet. As both fire and chorus die down, Roderigo and Iago join Cassio (tenor), the Captain of the Guard. Iago invites his companions to drink and although Cassio at first refuses (having drunk already) he finally capitulates in order to toast Otello and Desdemona. What ensues is a wonderful example of Verdi's genius for transforming the old into the new. Cassio praises the beauty and goodness of Desdemona—words which Iago uses to convince Roderigo that he has a rival—and then (prefaced by a sparkling orchestral introduction) Iago launches the *Brindisi*[4]. First he addresses Cassio, who replies in lines which complement Iago's both poetically and musically. The pattern is completed when Iago [5] sings the refrain (complete with his trill and a snaking chromatic scale) to be echoed by the chorus. A brief aside to Roderigo and the pattern is repeated: the same music but with the orchestra enriched by trills. The same aside ('*Un altro sorso e brillo egli e*', 'One more glass and he'll be drunk') is followed by the third strophe. The accompaniment is further enhanced—and so is the drama, for instead of the conventional completion of the pattern, Cassio, now very drunk, misses his cue and enters too soon. Instead of the expected refrain, the chorus laughs at the drunkard whilst Iago urges Roderigo to force a quarrel with Cassio, who staggers about and soon is brawling. Whilst Roderigo (at Iago's command) sounds the alarm, Montano (bass) (Otello's predecessor as Governor) intervenes and is wounded. The music becomes frantic; Otello enters ('*Abasso le spade!*' 'Your blades cast before me!'), and his recitative (strings with occasional, violent punctuation by the wind) calms the chaos. When Otello demands to know how the quarrel

14

arose, Iago disingenuously implies that Cassio is to blame. Disturbed by the noise, Desdemona (soprano) enters. Otello angrily dismisses Cassio from his post. He then gives brief orders which restore the peace and he and Desemona are left alone on stage.

Introduced by a muted solo cello with the other cellos divided, the superb love duet begins [6, 7, 8]. To words deftly woven from Acts One and Two of the play this gentle, tender, yearning and passionate duet captivates us by the sheer beauty of its sound—it also fully establishes the quality and depth of the relationship between Otello and Desdemona. The culmination is the sensually lovely passage [8] in which Otello thrice begs a kiss—we shall be brought back to this moment twice during the final act: it is on these kisses that the tragedy will hinge. Their recollection unifies the work and will achieve a special significance at the close of the opera. For the moment, with shimmering strings, harp and wind, and a final echo the duet's opening phrases, the duet completes the gigantic *decrescendo* which Verdi has constructed to occupy the whole act.

A dialogue between Cassio and Iago begins the second act. The richly developed orchestral introduction is based on a motif [9a] associated with Iago—at first fierce, later suave and charming, it is varied to suit his mood during this scene. Having suggested that the disconsolate Cassio ask Desdemona to intercede with Otello for his reinstatement, Iago bids his dupe depart ('*vanne*'), he then repeats this '*vanne*' in a much less friendly tone [9] and to a vicious unison outburst in the orchestra [10] he begins his satanic Creed. For this Boito expanded the merest hint in Shakespeare (where Iago, having advised Cassio to put his case to Desdemona, calls on the 'Divinity of Hell' while planning his next strategem) into a full-blooded, nihilistic declaration of evil. God is cruel; Man, created in God's image [11] is evil— a puppet of Fate. After the mockery of life comes death—and then? [10a] (*pp legato*). Nothing. Heaven is an ancient, idle tale [11]—complete with the full brass section braying derisive laughter. In Verdi's setting (riddled with trills, using a very wide dynamic range from *ppp* to *ff* and mostly declamatory vocal

Mariano Stabile as Iago. (Covent Garden Archives)

Lauritz Melchior as Otello. (Covent Garden Archives)

15

delivery) this electrifying piece displays an Iago far more positively evil than he is in Shakespeare, where his motivation rests on rumour and self-indoctrination, not on belief. The charm with which he continues his plot is chilling. Whilst Cassio approaches Desdemona, Iago drops casual words of suspicion which are overheard by Otello. He warns Otello [12] to beware of jealousy—poison is planted in four smooth phrases.

In its early stages Verdi had favoured calling the opera *Iago*. In a letter to his friend, the Neapolitan painter Domenico Morelli, he disagreed with the latter's view of Iago as a small, malicious figure and went on to reveal his own view of how Iago should be portrayed:

> . . . if I were an actor and had to play Iago, I would rather have a long, thin figure, thin lips, small eyes set close to the nose, like a monkey's, with broad, receding brow and the head developed behind; and an absent *nonchalant* manner, indifferent to everything, witty, speaking good and evil almost lightheartedly and having an air of indifference to what he says so that, if someone were to reproach him: 'What you say is vile!' he could answer: 'Really? I didn't think so . . . we'll say no more about it!' . . .
>
> A figure like this can deceive everyone, even—up to a point—his wife. A small, malicious figure arouses everyone's suspicion and deceives nobody! *Amen*.

In the distance Cassio has left Desdemona surrounded by Cypriots bringing her gifts of flowers and fruit [13]. The musical idiom now changes and at first seems strange. Some critics have dismissed this scene as overlong and dramatically superfluous. On the contrary, with its magically simple addition of mandolin, guitar and small bag-pipes to the orchestral accompaniment, it shows the simple beauty of Desdemona through the eyes of others, and its length is essential if the subsequent action is to prove credible. Desdemona's gracious qualities radiate as she echoes the greetings in soaring phrases (' *Splende il cielo* ' 'Heaven is smiling'): Otello is quite overcome and even Iago acknowledges her beauty, as he promises to destroy it. His opportunity comes all too soon. Desdemona approaches Otello and gently pleads Cassio's case [14]. Angrily he rejects her and casts away the handkerchief she proffers to his feigned headache. Their exchange grows into a masterly quartet [15] as Iago and Emilia (mezzo-soprano), Desdemona's maid, join the estranged couple. Iago snatches the handkerchief from Emilia and orders her silence—from it he will fabricate his evidence for the tragedy. The refinement of this quartet is extraordinary: the voices blend and exchange grouping subtly whilst the accompaniment both supports the voices and disturbs their languid lines with varied, quietly brittle figuration. Although Desdemona and Emilia leave, this accompaniment continues as Otello, emotionally exhausted, drops into a chair. Savouring the equivalent of Shakespeare's

> . . . I will in Cassio's lodging lose this napkin,
> And let him find it. Trifles light as air
> Are to the jealous confirmations strong
> As proofs of Holy writ . . .

Iago tucks the kerchief into his doublet. When he approaches Otello, the latter explodes in fury. So violent is his recitative (' *Tu? Indietro! fuggi!* ') that it overflows (rather than leads) into the aria [16] in which his spirit breaks. Despite its marching pulse and martial tone, snaking triplets slither its squareness away and invade Otello's vocal line. When Otello comes to a climax on a high B♭ and Iago bids him peace, the strings (*ppp molto staccato e tremolo*) are whipping continuous triplets as he demands proof, visual proof.

He is so overwrought that he seizes Iago by the throat.

With much show of reluctance, Iago makes sure that his poison runs fatally deep: once again using his most sensual voice he reports [17] a dream in which Cassio described his love for Desdemona and cursed the fate that gave her to the Moor. Flutes and oboe very quietly join the strings as Iago 'quotes' Cassio's words on a high repeated C which rises chromatically to D ('*Cauti vegliamo*' 'We must be careful') and then (chromatically!) slithers down an octave. His further 'quotation' (now darkened by clarinets, bassoon and horns) is delivered in a hollow, gloomy voice— despite the *dolcissimo* marking the 6/8 metre is shaken by gentle stresses on its weakest beats and the dream dissolves. The wondrous beauty of this narration, combined with the black falsity of its content breaks Otello completely: his response ('*Oh! mostruosa colpa*' 'Now I am sure she is guilty!') is softly spoken— stunned, he contemplates rather than condemns. When Iago offers him the proof of the handkerchief (which was Otello's first love-offering to Desdemona) 'seen' in Cassio's hand, violence surges back into Otello's voice (*ff*: '*Ah! mille vite gli donasse*') and triplet groups once more seize the accompaniment until Otello cuts it with his three insane cries for blood ('*Ah! sangue! sangue! sangue!*' 'Ah! Blood! Blood! Blood!'). Falling to his knees he swears vengeance to heaven. His part begins [18] on a monotone richly embroidered by wind. Iago prevents him from rising, and also kneels and swears. Only when they sing together (bringing the act to an heroic close) do we realise that it is Iago who has the melody— he quite literally 'calls the tune' whilst Otello accompanies the vocal line contrapuntally.

The most intricate counterpoint of the score opens Act Three mysteriously and, by using [12] as its thematic material, Verdi specifically recalls both Iago and jealousy. The music achieves a climax and subsides. After the herald's announcement (bass) of the Venetian ambassadors, Otello's single word, 'Continue', is thus directed both at Iago and the jealousy within his brooding mind. This act will see Otello's tortured doubt become (seeming) fact, for Iago undertakes to bring Cassio and provoke him into revealing his guilt. Just before Iago leaves he infuriates his victim with an insinuating '*il fazzoletto*' ('the handkerchief').

Desdemona's entry pours lyrical beauty on the scene [19] and throughout their exchange her affection contrasts with Otello's tense courtesy. She again pleads for Cassio and he demands the handkerchief repeatedly in ever-rising phrases. With dangerous insensitivity [20], she tries to return the conversation to Cassio. Abruptly Otello loses his self-control and challenges her to swear her innocence. Her protest of loyalty (expressed with the deepest feeling) infuriates him. Suddenly (as Verdi's directions instruct) he changes from rage to an icy irony which is far more terrifying. Citing her own music [19] he escorts her to the door where he brutally insults her as that 'vile, filthy harlot who's the wife of Otello', and ejects her from the room. Now utterly broken, he starts the opera's most painful aria on a brooding monotone. (Note how often the arias of this opera start on a monotone— and how much more powerfully expressive they are than the traditional *bel canto* lines). Meanwhile the orchestra doggedly pursues a small melodic figure through one harmonic and contrapuntal twist after another. With each change it gives new psychological power to the portrayal of Otello's saturated misery and hopeless efforts to escape his torment. This number is perhaps Verdi's greatest tragic achievement— nowhere is he so Wagnerian in the speaking power of the orchestra— and nowhere is he so profoundly Verdi, for, just at the right moment [21], the voice begins to rise and gradually launches on a slow, lyrical line as Otello sings of the eclipse of his sun, of the smile that had been his life's

17

greatest joy. Just when he curses his fate and declares that after proof there will be death, Iago returns: Cassio is here. The speed of the action is so great that Otello's line continues almost untouched and leads to a brief exchange of words after which Otello hides to listen and observe.

During the ensuing scene Iago talks to Cassio of Bianca (the latter's mistress). Their talk is somewhat ribald and rather jovial. Otello—now in, now out of earshot—naturally thinks that they refer to Desdemona and when the puzzled Cassio shows Iago the mysterious handkerchief he found in his rooms Iago waves it purposefully about: Otello sees it and his 'proof' is complete. The music Verdi writes here ([22] and [23] are but brief samples) is widely varied and unprecedented in its delicacy. This is the kind of texture which pervades his last opera *Falstaff* (written five years after *Otello*). Now a more formal tone intrudes as a solo trumpet rings out—others answer and the cannon shot announces the arrival of the embassy. Iago hustles Cassio away and whilst Cypriots call welcome to the Venetian ambassadors, Otello, at Iago's suggestion, decides to strangle Desdemona. Iago undertakes to despatch Cassio and Otello promotes him to the rank of Captain.

The grand ceremonial scene which follows has all the brilliance of the *auto-da-fé* in *Don Carlos* or the *Gran Finale secondo* in *Aida*. (It is interesting that when Verdi prepared Otello for the Paris production of 1894 it was here that he added the ballet music, as required by French operatic convention. Whilst dramatically superfluous, it parallels the treatment in *Aida* and has some scintillating music—and the six bars of *Invocation to Allah* have great dramatic strength.) Otello receives orders which recall him to Venice—Cassio is to succeed him as Governor of Cyprus! Goaded beyond endurance when he hears Desdemona tell Iago that she hopes to see Cassio and Otello reconciled, Otello publicly insults and strikes her (*A terra!... e piangi!...*) to the horror of the onlookers. Desdemona's exquisite lament [24] blossoms into a vast concerted number. This is static in its effect, but its size and brightness of scoring form a vivid foil against the dark-scored colouring of the final act. Also, within the number Iago eggs Otello on to vengeance and convinces Roderigo that he must kill Cassio or lose all hope of Desdemona. At a pause in the ensemble Otello turns on the crowd and commands them away. When Desdemona tries to comfort him, he curses her and collapses in a fit. Whilst Iago gloats over his triumph, the receding crowd praise Otello and the Lion of Venice. Iago (Verdi directs: 'with a gesture of horrible triumph') points at the prostrate body of Otello and sneers *'Ecco il Leone!'* ('There lies your lion!'). With a last, ironic shout from the crowd of 'Long live Otello', the curtain falls. Verdi substantially revised this finale for the first Paris performances in order to highlight Iago's words, which, despite his and the performers' efforts had not been sufficiently audible for him in the original score.

After the twisting cross-currents, swift action and public spectacle of the preceding acts, the last is simple in content: its whole action rests on the symmetry of the two deaths. The tone is dark and private. Wistfully and softly (in a dark G# minor) a cor anglais tries to lift a melodic phrase—it sinks away. Later the phrase will acquire words [27] as Desdemona sings the Willow Song, but now it is punctuated by flutes (the figure used in [25]—it will reappear for a full wind section later) and is answered by hollow sounding clarinets. Treated to thirty bars of chromatic and contrapuntal stretching, it seems an age before the curtain rises to reveal Emilia helping Desdemona in her preparation for bed. Desdemona's thoughts turn obsessively to death and a song which her mother's maid used to sing will not leave her mind (*'Mia madre aveva una povera ancella'* 'My mother once had a poor little maiden'). Plangently accompanied by the cor anglais, she sings this song of the willow

Gabrielle Krauss as Desdemona. She was compared to the great tragedienne Rachel for her acting genius. (Opera Rara)

[26] and [27] over and over again. The sense of circular repetition is oppressive but not monotonous because Verdi is careful to vary it with such touches as the portrayal of the gentle flight of birds ('*Scendean l'angelli a vol dai rami cupi*' 'From branches high above sweet birds came flying') or the sudden, frightening slap of a window in the wind. To heavy, sullen chords Desdemona bids her maid goodnight then, momentarily panic-stricken, she embraces Emilia [31] and says goodbye. The earlier figure [25] snakes back disturbingly. Its chromatic undulation shifts to a more restful A♭ major as Desdemona kneels before an icon of the Virgin Mary and says her prayer. The text of this *Ave Maria* is the final facet in the operatic portrayal of her personality. Her supplication grows to fervour [28], and then subsides before she goes to bed and sleep.

The dark orchestral colouring now darkens further as Otello enters the room. Only the double-bass section of the orchestra is used—and all except the leader of the section are muted. The music they play will later become [29], but here their three phrases are answered by the ominous sound of [30] played by cellos and followed by the thump of a *ppp* bass drum. These two elements struggle for dominance, but as Otello opens the bed curtains and gazes at the sleeping Desdemona ([29]—as played by cor anglais and bassoon over low, *tremolo* strings) the music slides into [8]; Otello kisses her three times. Almost before the shock of recollection grasps this huge sweeping reference backwards to the Act One duet it dissolves (deprived of its cadence) as Desdemona awakes. The figure of [30] now dominates the dialogue and becomes continuous as Otello suffocates his wife. Emilia gains entrance only to hear her dying mistress claim suicide to protect Otello:

19

Commend me to my kind lord: O farewell.
Furiously Otello accuses her of lying and himself admits the blame:
She's like a liar gone to burning hell:
'Twas I that killed her.

Emilia's cries bring others on the scene—only to reveal Iago's treachery and Otello's gullibility. Lodovico disarms the Moor. Otello quietly bids those present not to fear him: 'My journey's done. Otello's glory is vanished.' This replaces the miraculous nineteen lines in Shakespeare ('Soft you, a word or two before you go') in which Otello reviews his position as his own accuser, his own defending counsel, judge and executioner. In heart-rending lines (which return to an earlier passage in the play) he parts from his innocent, dead wife and stabs himself with a secreted dagger. Once again the music of [29] shadows the scene—and once again it flows into [8]. On the third kiss Otello dies (Verdi sets the last syllable beneath a rest: no pitched note, merely the expiring sound of speech) and this time the cadence (and the opera) is complete.

The full tragic effect of this ending devolves from much more than its immediate musical and dramatic substance. Much has been written of Verdi's re-use of the music of the love duet [8] and its effect here is precisely tragic since it locates Otello's *hubris* (his fatal pride) both at the moment of his greatest fulfilment (his love for Desdemona) and his destruction. Its overwhelming force cannot simply be explained by Verdi's use of a recollection theme (a common-place effect of Italian opera and of Verdi's own work, for instance in *La Forza del Destino* or *Aida*). Nor does it stem from the simple intensity Verdi injects into it (it is less simple than it seems and is further complicated by his other use of the same device at the start of Act Three [12]). By returning to Act One at this moment of tragic completion Verdi imposes a cyclic power onto the whole and forces us to re-examine the beginning in the light of the end. Why should he do this? The answer is both subtle and Shakespearean.

Shakespeare frequently equates particular images with critical dramatic motifs. In *Othello* Iago is equated with the Turk, and warfare (Othello's occupation) with the internal battle which will destroy him. Shakespeare first plays upon these motifs in Act Two Scene 1: *A sea port in Cyprus. An open place near the quay*. It took a good critic* nearly forty pages to explore the implications of this scene. Sagaciously Professor Goddard called it the 'Sixth Act of Othello' and described its 'silent music': that surface of activity which reveals its metaphysical core only after the tragedy is done. Verdi goes straight to this violent heart of darkness—the storm (*not* passing but to come) brings Otello who commands: 'Rejoice! The Turk's pride is buried in the sea; ours and heaven's is the glory! After our arms the storm destroyed him.' Not so, said Shakespeare; and even more directly Verdi says the same: the storm is only beginning and that 'Turk' is neither buried nor destroyed. This is the structural dynamo which drives the tragedy—hence the reason Verdi writes so huge an opening storm. This has nothing in common with those pretty orchestral parentheses which litter the operatic repertory. By the time it seems to have died down (that huge act-lasting *decrescendo*) we know the people of a tragedy which only then (in those three kisses) begins. A later poet was to say (himself quoting the motto of a tragic Queen)— *In my beginning is my end*: it is time for the curtain to go up on Verdi's greatest drama.

*Harold G. Goddard— *The Meaning of Shakespeare* (The University of Chicago Press, 1951)

Leo Slezak (Otello) and Frances Alda (Desdemona); Slezak alone rivalled Tamagno's interpretation and sang the part regularly at the Metropolitan between 1909 and 1913. The opera was then not heard there until 1937 (Martinelli). (Stuart-Liff Collection)

Verdi with Maurel, the first Iago, backstage at the Paris Opéra on the occasion of the Paris premiére. (Stuart-Liff Collection)

Verdi, Shakespeare, and the Italian audience

William Weaver

In 1865, after the mixed reception of his *Macbeth* in Paris, Verdi was stung by some of the criticisms and impelled to write a letter, now famous, defending his comprehension of Shakespeare. 'I may not have set *Macbeth* well,' the composer wrote, 'but to say that I do not know, do not understand, and do not feel Shakespeare — no, by God, no. He is a poet of whom I am particularly fond. I have had his works in my hands since my earliest youth. I read and re-read him constantly.'

The key words in this passage are 'in my hands', *tra le mani*. Verdi had grown up reading Shakespeare, but it was not until he visited England in 1847, at the time of *I Masnadieri's* première at Her Majesty's Theatre, that he actually saw a play of Shakespeare performed. Earlier that same year, he had completed and staged his *Macbeth*, in its first version, in Florence; he knew the play only from the printed page, from the several Italian translations already published. Until the second half of the 19th century, in fact, Shakespeare — for the Italians — was a poet to be read, not to be seen. Thus, in bringing *Macbeth* to the Italian stage, Verdi had been boldly innovative.

Shakespeare reached the Italian theatre by way of the opera house. Verdi's *Macbeth*, though it seems to have been the first opera based on that tragedy, was far from being the first Italian opera of Shakespearean inspiration. The earlier operas, however, unlike Verdi's, seldom came directly from the poet's text. Often (and Rossini's *Otello* is a case in point) the works stemmed from imitations of Shakespeare, notably those of the French neo-classical actor and dramatist Jean-François Ducis (1733-1816), whose *Hamlet* and *Othello* are essentially very free variations on Shakespearean themes (they were translated also into Italian and occasionally peformed). Other operas, including Bellini's *I Capuleti ed i Montecchi* and Gasparini's *Amleto*, were derived not from Shakespeare but from his same sources.

Felice Romani, the most fertile and erudite Italian librettist of the early 19th century, provided an *Amleto* for Mercadante in 1823. Romani had a penchant for Prefaces and he provided one for the printed text of his opera, first outlining the plot: 'The old King of Denmark is treacherously murders by his wife Geltrude, who is madly in love with her kinsman Claudio...' In this *Amleto*, as in others that followed it in Italian opera houses, the theme of fratricide is firmly avoided.

Summing up, Romani says: 'This is the subject of the present opera based on the plots of Shakespeare and of his imitator Ducis.

'It is fairly well known that Hamlet is the Orestes of the North, Claudius is the Aegisthus, and Gertrude, the Clytemnestra; for this reason, the poet has modelled the characters of these three on those of the Greeks. In this fashion, he felt they could be made, if not more interesting, at least more suited to our stage than they are in the English original, which is a bit too fantastic, and in the copy by Ducis, which he feels is too weak and colourless.'

It is hard to find much that is Greek in this *Amleto* (except for the Prince's occasional mention of the Furies), or much that is Shakespearean. But there is much that is conventionally operatic, from the opening chorus and *festa* for Claudio's coronation to Geltrude's final cabaletta and death scene, at which the appeased ghost appears to Amleto, who survives the carnage.

A confirmed classicist, Romani regarded Shakespeare with some misgivings; still, the English poet obviously fascinated the Italian librettist. In 1834 Romani supplied Mercadante with another text with Shakespearean ingredients: *La gioventu di Enrico quinto* (*The young manhood of Henry V*). Like nearly all Romani's librettos, this one was adapted from an earlier work, set (in Italian) by the French composer Ferdinand Hérold in 1815. But while the text of Hérold's popular work had nothing to do with Shakespeare, Romani introduced into his version a supremely Shakespearean character, Falstaff, and adapted two scenes — quite extraneous to the plot — from the *Henry* plays.

Less than a year after Verdi's first *Macbeth* the Teatro la Fenice in Venice presented another *Amleto*, in 1848. The music was by Antonio Buzzola on a libretto by Giovanni Peruzzini, who also wrote a Preface to the printed verses. 'Anyone who knows *Hamlet*, the sublime creation of Shakespeare,' Peruzzini writes, 'can easily see how it is anything but adaptable to the restricted form of the "dramma per musica". But even if it were, I would have avoided using it, as a profanation. I declare therefore that from the *Hamlet* of the sublime Englishman, I have taken almost nothing save the name [...] I felt I could rightfully imagine, on my own, dramatic situations suited to the rather grandiose and fantastic genre of modern music.'

Note: now it is modern music that has become fantastic. A generation earlier, in his own *Amleto* preface, Romani had accused Shakespeare of being too fantastic for modern opera. And, for that matter, Verdi's *Macbeth* had just been criticized for being in the 'fantastic' vein by no less an authority than the poet Giuseppe Giusti, who had urged Verdi to return to the Italian — that is to say, patriotic — subjects of his triumphant early works.

In 1854, again in Venice, but at the Teatro Gallo rather than the Fenice, there was yet another *Amleto*, in the very season that witnessed the Gallo's spectacularly successful revival of *La Traviata*, a near-fiasco at the Fenice the year before. At this period, Venetian censorship was severe, as Verdi had had occasion to learn when preparing *Rigoletto*, also for the Fenice, in 1851. The severity of the Austrian authorities is perhaps reflected in the *Amleto* libretto by Angelo Zanardini, who was also the work's composer. Here there is no mention of Denmark or of thrones: regicide is taboo. Claudius becomes simply Alstano, count of Elsinoro; and Zanardini is as far from Shakespeare as most of his predecessors were. The ending of the opera is characteristic: Claudius and Gertrude (alias Alstano and Adelia) repent, are pardoned by Amleto, then ascend the scaffold together, to the strains of a funeral march. Amleto, again, survives.

While, in these aberrant forms, Shakespeare was growing more and more familiar to the opera audience, his plays were making a timid entrance into the Italian spoken theatre. In the mid-1840s, the great Gustavo Modena, ardent patriot and much-admired actor, made a brave, but unsuccessful attempt to stage *Othello*. Accounts of the event make curious reading today. Italian audiences of the time were accustomed to comedy or to tragedy, but not to any contamination of the two; and so the Milanese public at this *Othello* was first bewildered, then outraged. Some years later, Modena related the reception of the first scene to his young colleague Ernesto Rossi: 'When the curtain had gone up, after the usual Overture, at the scene between Iago and Rodrigo, when the latter begins to shout from the street: "What, ho, Brabantio! [...]", the public began to mutter: What is this, a tragedy or a farce? And when Brabantio finally appears on the balcony, half-asleep [...] the public began to laugh and to hiss'. Before the scene could end, the audience had grown so violent that Modena was forced to ring down the curtain. For almost a decade there were no further Shakespearean ventures on the Italian stage.

Then, in the spring of 1856, again in Milan, Rossi produced *Othello* at the Teatro Re and enjoyed an immense success. His memoirs tell us: 'The approval was generous and spontaneous. Othello had aroused in the spectators far more pity than terror. The audience left the theatre moved by the sad end of Desdemona, but they wept for the hapless fate of Othello [...] Shakespeare was no longer a barbarian, and people began to consider him a human poet'.

Two weeks later Rossi repeated his success with *Hamlet*, and soon his Shakespeare productions — *Hamlet* in particular — were a regular, cherished part of the Italian theatrical season. Other actors and actresses of renown soon followed his lead; and the Italian repertory underwent a drastic change. Italian Shakespeare — by Rossi or by Adelaide Ristori or by Tommaso Salvini — became a significant cultural export.

At the time of those first Rossi Shakespeare performances in Milan, Arrigo Boito was fourteen, a student at the Milan Conservatory. A precocious, if not always docile student, his interests ranged far beyond music, and far beyond Italy, so it is quite likely that, young as he was, he nevertheless attended those revolutionary productions.

Seven years later, after he had won his diploma from the Conservatory and—in Paris—had completed his first collaboration with Verdi, on the *Hymn of the Nations*, Boito embarked on the writing of a libretto for his friend Franco Faccio. His choice was Shakesperean: the operatically popular *Amleto*.

But Boito's libretto is on an entirely different level from those of Romani, Peruzzini, and Zanardini. Though his command of English was shaky, his *Amleto* is the most Shakespearean libretto to appear in Italian opera since Verdi's *Macbeth* almost a generation before; and it is unquestionably the best Shakespeare-inspired libretto until Boito's own *Otello* a generation later.

By now, the librettist could rely to some extent on the audience's knowledge of the play. Besides the numerous performances of *Hamlet* by Rossi and others, there had also been new translations (internal evidence suggests Boito relied heavily on Giulio Carcano's verse translation).

Of course, Boito had to make cuts: most of the secondary characters are omitted; but he retained the grave-diggers who—comic elements in a tragedy—would have been inadmissible on the opera stage in the 1840s, when Verdi had to eliminate the Drunken Porter from *Macbeth*. As a member of the 'scapigliatura' school, the 'dishevelled' poets and painters influenced by Baudelaire, Boito took delight in shocking his elders; and so in the first act of *Amleto* Claudio sings a blasphemous Brindisi: 'Peace to the dead, and let the cup be filled with restoring drink. Let us pray for them, and let the chalice spill over the altar'. Again, in Act Three, in a monologue based on Shakespeare's 'O my offence is rank', Claudio recites a Pater Noster with irreverent interjections, a foretaste of Iago's ironic Credo in the Boito-Verdi *Otello*.

For the play scene, universally excised by previous librettists, Boito introduces some singers, who perform a succinct but effective 'murder opera', arousing contrasting reactions in the divided chorus (a device surely drawn from Gozzi and used by Prokofiev in his *Love of Three Oranges*). The choral dispute echoes the wrangling of the conservatives and progressives, the Wagnerites and the nationalists, in the musical Milan of the 1860s.

As more plays of Shakespeare entered the repertory, Shakespearean operas continued to be written. The composer Filippo Marchetti presented a *Romeo e Giulietta* in 1865, and Ciro Pinsuti (largely British-trained) composed, in 1873, a *Mercante di Venezia*, with the usual Preface by the librettist, G.T. Cimino: 'the distinguished composer [...] has decided that the fairytale conceived by the sublime Englishman, rich in honest and generous affections, is more worthy than the usual torments of daggers and scaffolds, suicides, uxoricides, poisonings, conspiracies, and other such horrors, illuminated by flashes of electric light, decorated with processions of monks and nuns [. . .]'.

Worthy or not, the Cimino-Pinsuti *Merchant* is depressingly banal (and the audience must have longed for a good uxoricide and an explosion of electric lightning), distinguished only by its ferocious anti-semitism, which surpasses that of the original.

The question of fidelity or infidelity to Shakespeare in the opera house must be considered in the light of the now-frequent legitimate performances of Shakespeare in Italy. These, in the latter decades of the 19th century, are well-documented, and the accounts reveal a considerable—if understandable—licence on the part of the actor-managers, often responsible for making or adapting the translation. In its conscious competition with the more popular opera house, the legitimate theatre encouraged highly 'operatic' versions of Shakespeare's plays (thus the surviving acting copy of Rossi's *Macbeth* shows infiltrations from Piave's libretto for Verdi). Cuts were frequent, and so were interpolations.

Still, even as far as these practices were concerned, times started to change. In the early 1880s, when Bioto was preparing his *Otello* libretto, he felt free to surpress an entire act, to cut, to add vital pages, such as the Credo. Then, only a few years later, in preparing a translation of *Anthony and Cleopatra* for Eleonora Duse, at the height of her early career (and at the height of her love affair with Boito), the Italian writer took similar liberties, condensing and adjusting the drama until it was hardly more than a vehicle for the leading lady. He did not get away with it. The critics, willing to accept certain freedoms in the opera house, were less tolerant in the spoken theatre. This was no longer the Italy of the 1850s. Boito's version of *Anthony and Cleopatra* was roundly condemned, somewhat to his amazement; Duse gave only a limited number of performances in Italy, took it abroad, then dropped it.

Boito's libretto for *Falstaff* is, of course, another story. In this instance, it was based largely on a work— *The Merry Wives of Windsor*—practically unknown to Italian audiences and virtually incomprehensible to Italian readers. This time, Boito did not merely take liberties: he asserted his total independence, and forged a new piece from old materials.

In the decades since the second World War, Shakespeare's place in the Italian theatre has been enhanced by remarkable translations by such poets as Giuseppe Ungaretti, Eugenio Montale, Salvatore Quasimono, and by productions mounted by Luchino Visconti, Giorgio Strehler, and others. At the same time, the gradual rediscovery of the early Verdi canon has brought the composer's *Macbeth* back to the opera house, along with his *Otello* and *Falstaff*. So now, Shakespeare and Verdi, drama and opera, are rightfully partners in the world of the Italian theatre.

Thematic Guide

Many of the themes from the opera have been identified in the articles by numbers in square brackets, which refer to the themes set out on these pages. The themes are also identified by the numbers in brackets at the corresponding points in the libretto, so that the words can be related to the musical themes.

[1] CHORUS

Allegro agitato

God, whose an - ger roused this tem - pest!
Dio, ful - gor del - la bu - fer - ra!

[2] OTELLO

Allegro agitato

O re - joice now! The glo - ry of the Moslems has drown'd at sea
E - sul - ta - te! L'or - go - glio mu-sul -ma - no se-pol to è in mar,

[3] IAGO

Allegro assai moderato

Those fra - gile vows that a wo - man swore
Se un fra - gil vo - to di fe - mi - na

[4] *Brindisi*/IAGO

Allegro con brio

Good com - rades brave and true
In - naf - fia l'u - go - la!

drink up, drink deep - ly!
Trin - ca, tra - can - na!

[5] *Brindisi/* **IAGO**

Allegro con brio

So raise your glass - es and sing a - gain to the
Chi al - l'e - sca'ha mor - so del di - ti - ram - bo spa -

old re - frain of be - va con me,
val - do e stram - bo be - va con me,

[6] **OTELLO**

Cantabile

Now in the si - lent dark - ness the strife is heard no more
Già nel - la not - te den - sa s'e - stin - gue o - gni cla - mor.

[7] **OTELLO**

Ah, how you loved me for those woes I'd suf - fered
E tu m'a - ma - vi per le mie sven - tu - re

[8]

Cantabile

con espressione

[9] *Credo/* **IAGO**

Allegro

Take it,
Van - ne;

take the path to your ru - in.
la tua me - ta già ve - do.

[10] *Credo*/IAGO

Allegro sostenuto

Yes, I be - lieve in God
Cre - do in un Dio cru - del

[11]

Allegro sostenuto

f   aspro

[12] IAGO

Moderato *cupo e legato*

Fear that blind mon - ster, jea - lous - y, jea - lous - y,
Eu - n'i - dra fo - sca, li - vi - da, cie - ca,

[13] CHORUS

Allegro moderato

pp dolce

At your glances flame in our hearts   leaps up to   meet you.
Do - ve guar - di splen - do - no rag -   gi av - vam - pan   cuo - ri

[14] DESDEMONA

Allegro moderato

I come from some - one who has felt your an - ger
D'un uom che ge - me sot - to il tuo di - sde - gno

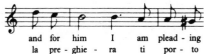

and for him I am plead - ing
la pre - ghie - ra ti por - to

29

[15] **DESDEMONA**

Largo

calmo

Grant me O grant me sweet words of par - don say you for - give me
Dam - mi la dol - ce e lie - ta pa - ro - la del per - do - no

[16] **OTELLO**

Allegro assai ritenuto *larga la frase*

p

Now and for - ev - er fare - well
O - ra e per sem - pre ad - dio

all that I lived for
san - te me - mo - rie

[17] **IAGO**

Andantino

pp

Dark - ness had fall - en, Cas - sio was sleep- ing, I lay be - side him
E - ra la not - te, Cas - sio dor- mi, a gli sta -vo ac- can - to

[18] **OTELLO**

Molto sostenuto

solenne *f*

See me swear, you heav'ns a - bove me
Si, pel ciel mar - mo - reo giu - ro

[19] **DESDEMONA**

Allegro moderato

God give you joy my hus- band, dear lord and ru - ler of my heart
Dio ti gio-con- di, o spo - so, del-l'al-ma mia so- vra - no.

30

[20] **DESDEMONA**

Andantino *con eleganza*

You are try - ing to tease me,
Tu di me ti fai gio - co,

[21] **OTELLO**

Adagio *cantabile*

But, oh pain, oh grief! I have
Ma, o pian - to, o duol! m'han ra -

lost my fair vis - ion
pi - to il mi - rag - gio

[22]

Allegro moderato

[23] **IAGO**

Allegro brillante

Love is a spi - der cun - ning and wise
Que - sta è u - na ra - gna do - ve il tuo cuor

[24] **DESDEMONA**

Cantabile

One day my life was smi - ling when love and hope in - spired me
E un dì sul mio sor - ri - so fio - ria la spe - me e il ba - cio

[25] *The Willow Song* / **DESDEMONA**

Andante mosso

p con espressione

31

[26]

[27] **DESDEMONA**

The poor soul sat sigh - ing, be - neath a wil - low
Pian - ge - a can - tan - do nel - l'er - ma lan - da,

[28] **DESDEMONA**

dolce Pray | — for those who hum - bly kneel be - fore thee,
Pre - ga per chi a - do - ran - do a te, si pro - stra,

[29]

[30]

pp e staccate

[31] **OTELLO**

Do not fear me, tho' I still have my sword here!
Niun mi te - ma, se an coar - ma - to mi ve - de.

Otello

A lyric drama in four acts

Music by Giuseppe Verdi
Libretto by Arrigo Boito
English translation by Andrew Porter

This libretto is based on Boito's published libretto, rather than the vocal score which sometimes differs in tiny details. The stage directions are a literal translation of the original ones, which were authorised by Verdi and Boito and form a more or less intrinsic part of their conception; they do not form part of Andrew Porter's translation of the text made for the 1981 ENO production. This text of the translation also retains the word contractions which are necessary for setting words below notes in the vocal score, although the translator would have preferred them to be spelt out fully in the printed text. Exclamations such as 'Oh' and laughter such as 'Ha! Ha!' have been printed in accordance with Italian rather than English convention, in both languages, as 'O' and 'Ah! Ah!'. The numbers in square brackets relate to the thematic guide.

The first performance of *Otello* was at La Scala, Milan, on February 5, 1887. It was first heard in New York on April 16, 1888 and in London at the Lyceum Theatre on July 5, 1889.

It is inevitable that alterations will be made to any performing translation of a libretto in the course of rehearsals, during performances and in revival. In order to make this book available for the first performances scheduled by ENO, it has been necessary to go to print before the translator had the usual and necessary opportunities to finalise his translation.

THE CHARACTERS

Otello *a Moor, General of the Venetian forces*	Tenor
Iago *his ensign* (Jago)	Baritone
Cassio *a captain*	Tenor
Roderigo *a Venetian gentleman*	Tenor
Lodovico *Ambassador of the Venetian Republic*	Bass
Montano *Otello's predecessor as Governor of Cyprus*	Bass
A Herald	Bass
Desdemona *wife of Otello*	Soprano
Emilia *wife of Iago*	Mezzo-Soprano

Soldiers and sailors of the Venetian Republic; Venetian ladies and gentlemen; Cypriot men, women and children; men of the Greek, Dalmatian and Albanian armies; an inn-keeper and his four servers; seamen.

Place: A seaport in Cyprus.
Time: The end of the fifteenth century.

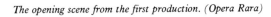

The opening scene from the first production. (Opera Rara)

Opens on Cyprus — skips Venice ✓

Act One

The castle exterior. A tavern with pergola. Downstage bastions and the sea. It is a stormy night, with thunder and lightning.
Scene One. *Iago, Roderigo, Cassio, Montano, and later, Otello, Cypriots and Venetian soldiers.*

CHORUS (TENORS)
See, the sail there!   Una vela!

CHORUS (BASSES)
See, the sail there!   Una vela!

FIRST GROUP
See the banner!   Un vessillo!

SECOND GROUP
See the banner!   Un vessillo!

MONTANO
It's the Lion of St Mark!   È l'alato Leon!

CASSIO
Now the lightning reveals her.   Or la folgor lo svela.

(*Trumpets sound on stage.*)

CHORUS (TENORS)
Hear the trumpet!   Uno squillo!

CHORUS (BASSES)
(*joining the others*)
Hear the trumpet!   Uno squillo!

(*A cannon shot is heard.*)

CHORUS (TENORS AND BASSES)
And the gun gives reply!   Ha tuonato il cannon!

CASSIO
It's the ship of the general.   È la nave del Duce.

MONTANO
Upward heaving.   Or s'affonda.
Plunging wildly...   Or s'inciela...

CASSIO
Through the waves she is cleaving.   Erge il rostro dall'onda.

CHORUS
She is lost in the storm and the night   Nelle nubi si cela e nel mar
But the lightning reveals her to sight.   E alla luce dei lampi ne appar.

ALL

Lightning! Thunder! Whirlwinds! Fury of the raging thunderbolt!	Lampi! tuoni! gorghi! turbi tempestosi e fulmini!
Waves are heaving! Winds are howling! Both the sea and the mountains quake.	Treman l'onde, treman l'aure, treman basi e culmini.

(*Townswomen enter upstage.*)

Through the air some gloomy spectre seems to rush and threaten us,	Fende l'etra un torvo e cieco—spirto di vertigine,
As if God would shake the heavens, shake them like a veil.	Iddio scuote il cielo bieco,—come un tetro vel.
All is darkness! All's aflame now! Boiling pitch enshrouds the sea	Tutto è fumo! tutto è fuoco! l'orrida caligine
And sky blazes, then it dies and all is darkness. Both sea and	Si fa incendio, poi si spegne più funesta, spasima
Land are shaken, the wind is howling through the waves and lashing them,	L'universo, accorre a valchi—l'aquilon fantasima,
There's a sound of demon clarions pealing in the sky.	I titanici oricalchi—squillano nel ciel.

ALL
(*with gestures of fright and supplication, facing towards the bastion*)

God whose anger aroused this tempest! [1]	Dio, fulgor della bufera!
God whose smile can calm its fury!	Dio, sorriso della duna!
Save, oh save that gallant vessel	Salva l'arca e la bandiera
Bearing the hero who can save us!	Della veneta fortuna!

35

God, the wind and waves obey you!	Tu, che reggi gli astri e il Fato!
God, you rule both sea and sky!	Tu, che imperi al mondo e al ciel!
Grant that shelter'd in our harbour,	Fa che in fondo al mar placato
She may at anchor safely lie!	Posi l'àncora fedel.

IAGO

The mainsail's split in two!	È infranto l'artimon!

RODERIGO

Toward the cliff	Il rostro piomba
The vessel is hurtling!	Su quello scoglio!

CHORUS

O save her! O save her!	Aita! Aita!

IAGO
(*to Roderigo*)

Let angry	L'alvo
Breakers smash the ship and drown her gen'ral!	Frenetico del mar sia la sua tomba!

CHORUS

She's safe now! She's safe now!	È salvo! salvo!

OFF-STAGE VOICES

Prepare to man the row-boats!	Gittate i palischermi!
Hands to the halyards! Haul there!	Mano alle funi! Fermi!

CHORUS (TENORS)

Man the shore boats!	Forza ai remi!

CHORUS (BASSES)
(*descending the bastion stairway*)

To the harbour!	Alla riva!…

OFF-STAGE VOICES

Man the quay! We are landing!	All'approdo! allo sbarco!
Man the shore! We are landing!	Ancorate il vascello!

OTHER OFF-STAGE VOICES

Evviva! Evviva!	Evviva! Evviva!

OTELLO
(*climbing to the bastion by the stairs from the beach followed by sailors and soldiers*)

O rejoice now! The glory of the Moslems [2]	Esultate! L'orgoglio musulmano
Has drowned at sea, we by God's aid are victorious!	Sepolto è in mar, nostra e del ciel è gloria!
What our arms spared, the sea and storm have vanquished.	Dopo l'armi lo vinse l'uragano.

ALL

Evviva Otello! Vittoria! Vittoria!	Evviva Otello! Vittoria! Vittoria!

(*Otello enters the fortress, followed by Cassio, Montano and soldiers.*)

CHORUS

Victorious! Destruction!	Vittoria! Sterminio!
All shattered and broken,	Dispersi, distrutti,
They lie in the sea below	Sepolti nell' orrido
Deep under the wave.	Tumulto piombâr.
To sing them a requiem	Avranno per requie
The ocean will thunder,	La sferza dei flutti,
And lashed by the hurricane	La ridda dei turbini,
They lie in the sea far below.	L'abisso del mar.

CHORUS

A calm succeeds the storm now.	Si calma la bufera.

IAGO
(*aside to Roderigo*)

Roderigo,	Roderigo,
Speak up, what are you thinking?	Ebben, che pensi?

RODERIGO

I shall drown myself…	D'affogarmi…

Act I Scene i in play — takes place in V[e]
Rod. & Iago say that O & D eloped. R[a]
to marry D.

36

(Much activity takes place upstage as the seamen climb the stairway from the beach and enter the castle carrying arms and baggage, while townspeople emerge from behind the fortress carrying branches to make a fire by the bastion. Soldiers with torches illuminate the way for the townspeople.)

IAGO

Fool… no one	Stolto
Should drown himself for the love of woman.	È chi s'affoga per amor di donna.

RODERIGO

What should I do?	Vincer nol so.

(At one side some bystanders stack a pile of wood while the rest of the crowd gathers round, inquisitive and noisy.)

IAGO

Take heart, be patient, believe me,	Suvvia, fa senno, aspetta
Time is on your side; for the lovely Desdemona,	L'opra del tempo. A Desdemona bella,
Who fills your secret dreams with tender longing,	Che nel segreto dei tuoi sogni adori,
Will be tired very soon of black embraces	Presto in uggia verranno i foschi baci
And brutal kisses from that thick-lipped savage.	Di quel selvaggio dalle gonfie labbra.
Good Roderigo, I love you most sincerely,	Buon Roderigo, amico tuo sincero
You must believe me; I can see your [3] suffering	Mi ti professo, né in più forte ambascia
And I know how to help. Those fragile vows	Soccorrerti potrei. Se un fragil voto
That a woman swore should prove an easy knot	Di femmina non è tropp'arduo nodo
For me to untie with hell to help me; you shall	Pel genio mio né per l'inferno, giuro
Enjoy that woman as your own. Now listen,	Che quella donna sarà tua. M'ascolta:
Though it seems that I love him, I hate Otello…	Bench'io finga d'amarlo, odio quel Moro…

(Enter Cassio. He joins a group of soldiers. Iago aside to Roderigo.)

A reason for my hatred, there it is, see him.	…E una cagion dell'ira, eccola, guarda

(pointing to Cassio)

That debonair and dapper captain usurps	Quell'azzimato capitano usurpa
The rank that's mine, the rank that's mine; in many a	Il grado mio, il grado mio che in cento
Well-fought furious battle richly I earned it.	Ben pugnate battaglie ho meritato;

(The sailors continue to mill about upstage)

Such was the will of Otello; and I continue to	Tal fu il voler d'Otello, ed io rimango
Serve his noble Moorish Lordship as ensign!	Di sua Moresca signoria l'alfiere!

(Ever-thickening columns of smoke rise from the fire.)

But just as surely as your name's Roderigo,	Ma, come è ver che tu Roderigo sei,
I can assure you that if I were Otello,	Così è pur vero che se il Moro io fossi
I'd fear to have around me a man like Iago.	Vedermi non vorrei d'attorno un Jago.
Now listen closely…	Se tu m'ascolti…

(Iago leads Roderigo downstage. The fire blazes up. The soldiers crowd around the tables of the tavern.)

CHORUS

(During the song around the warming fire, the inn-keeper and his servers hang up around the pergola coloured Venetian lanterns which gaily illuminate the scene. The soldiers gather around the tables, some sitting, others standing, chatting and drinking.)

Flame of rejoicing!—merrily burning	Fuoco di gioia!—i'ilare vampa
Turning the night to glorious day.	Fuga la notte—col suo splendor,
Shining and sparkling, crackling and blazing,	Guizza, sfavilla,—crepita, avvampa,
Filling the heart with fiery joy.	Fulgido incendio—che invade il cor.

Drawn by the firelight fair shapes assemble,   Dal raggio attratti—vaghi sembianti
Moving around us changing their form,   Movono intorno—mutando stuol.
Now like fair maidens in graceful chorus,   E son fanciulle—dai lieti canti,
And then like butterflies with wings aflame,   E son farfalle—dall'igneo vol.
The palmwood sparkles, the cedar gives   Arde la palma—col sicomoro,
      answer,
Like faithful lovers singing of love,   Canta la sposa—col suo fedel;
On golden flicker, on cheerful chorus   Sull'aurea fiamma,—sul lieto coro
The gentle breezes waft from above.   Soffia l'ardente—spiro del ciel.
Flame of rejoicing rapidly blazing,   Fuoco di gioia—rapido brilla!
Rapidly dying fire of love!   Rapido passa—fuoco d'amor!
Gleaming and glowing, flickering and   Splende, s'oscura—palpita, oscilla,
      fading,
One final sparkle leaps up and dies.   L'ultimo guizzo—lampeggia e muor.

(*Gradually the fire dies down. The storm subsides. Iago, Roderigo, Cassio and several other soldiers stand or sit around a table drinking.*)

IAGO

Roderigo, drink up! Raise your glass,   Roderigo, beviam! qua la tazza,
My gallant captain.   Capitano.

CASSIO

    I'll drink no more.   Non bevo più.

IAGO
(*moving the wine jug towards Cassio's glass*)
    Your glass   Ingoia
Should not be empty.   Questo sorso.

CASSIO
(*withdrawing his glass*)
    No.   No.

IAGO
    Captain! We must celebrate   Guarda! oggi impazza
The triumph! It's a night of rejoicing,   Tutta Cipro! è una notte di gioia,
Therefore...   Dunque...

CASSIO
    Leave me. Already I'm dizzy   Cessa. Già m'arde il cervello
After one single glassful.   Per un nappo vuotato.

IAGO
    Well, that means you   Si, ancora
Need another. To the nuptials of Otello   Bever devi. Alle nozze d'Otello
And Desdemona.   E Desdemona!

ALL
(*except Roderigo*)
    Evviva!   Evviva!

CASSIO
(*lifting the cup to his lips and sipping the wine*)
    She makes lovely   Essa infiora
This island.   Questo lido.

IAGO
(*sottovoce to Roderigo*)
    (You hear him.)   (Lo ascolta.)

CASSIO
    To beauty   Col vago
Such as hers ev'ry heart must surrender.   Suo raggiar chiama i cuori a raccolta.

RODERIGO
Yet withal she is modest.   Pur modesta essa è tanto.

CASSIO
    You, Iago,   Tu, Jago,
Sing a song in her praises!   Canterai le sue lodi!

IAGO
(*to Roderigo*)
    (You hear him.)   (Lo ascolta.)
(*in a loud voice to Cassio*)
What am I but a critic?   Io non sono che un critico.

CASSIO

And far beyond

All praise is her beauty.

D'ogni lode è più bella.   Ed ella

IAGO

(*in the same way, aside to Roderigo*)

(Be careful

Of that Cassio.

Da quel Cassio.   (Ti guarda

RODERIGO

Why careful?   Che temi?

IAGO

(*becoming more and more insistent*)

You heard his   Ei favella

Ardent lyrical words, passionate youth will	Già con troppo bollor, la gagliarda
Spur him on to adventure; he's a smooth and	Giovinezza lo sprona; è un astuto
Clever charmer and he'll be your rival.	Seduttor che t'ingombra il cammino.
Watch him...	Bada...

RODERIGO

And then?   Ebben?

IAGO

If he's drunk he is ruined!   S'ei s'inebria è perduto!

Make him drink.)   Fallo ber.)

(*to the servers*)

Hey, attend us, some wine here!   Qua, ragazzi, del vino!

Iago fills the three glasses: one for himself, one for Roderigo and one for Cassio. The servers go from table to table with their wine-jugs. Iago addresses Cassio, with glass in hand: the crowd approach, and look at him with curiosity./ Brindisi

Good comrades, brave and true,	[4] Innaffia l'ugola!
Drink up, drink deeply!	Trinca, tracanna!
Life soon will pass away,	Prima che svampino
Drink while you can.	Canto e bicchier.

CASSIO

(*to Iago, with glass in hand*)

Come let me fill my glass	Questa del pampino
With golden nectar	Verace manna
That drives gloomy clouds away	Di vaghe annugola
From heart of man.	Nebbie il pensier.

IAGO

(*to all*)

So raise your glasses	[5] Chi all'esca ha morso
And sing again to	Del ditirambo
The old refrain of	Spavaldo e strambo
'Beva con me!'	Beva con me!

CHORUS

We raise our glasses	[5] Chi all'esca ha morso
And sing again to	Del ditirambo
The old refrain of	Spavaldo e strambo
'Beva con me!'	Beva con te!

IAGO

(*softly to Roderigo, indicating Cassio*)

(One more glass   (Un altro sorso

And he'll be drunk.)   E brillo egli è.)

RODERIGO

(*to Iago*)

(One more glass   (Un altro sorso

And he'll be drunk.)   E brillo egli è.)

IAGO

(*in a loud voice*)

The world goes whirling round	Il mondo palpita
When I am drinking!	Quand'io son brillo!
Then I defy ev'ry	Sfido l'ironico
Danger Fate can bring!	Nume e il destin!

CASSIO

(*still drinking*)

Tuned like a mandolin   Come un armonico

39

With music I sway; when
I hear that joyful sound
I sway and sing!

Liuto oscillo;
La gioia scalpita
Sul mio cammin!

IAGO
(*as above*)

So raise your glasses
And sing again to
The old refrain of
'Beva con me!'

Chi all'esca ha morso
Del ditirambo
Spavaldo e strambo
Beva con me!

ALL

We raise our glasses
And sing again to
The old refrain of
'Beva con me!'

Chi all'esca ha morso
Del ditirambo
Spavaldo e strambo
Beve con te.

IAGO
(*to Roderigo*)

(One more glass
And he'll be drunk.)

(Un altro sorso
E brillo egli è.)

RODERIGO
(*to Iago*)

(One more glass
And he'll be drunk.)

(Un altro sorso
E brillo egli è.)

IAGO
(*in a loud voice*)

He who despises good
Wine is a coward.
His heart conceals deadly
Secrets...

Fuggan dal vivido
Nappo i codardi
Che in cor nascondono
Frodi...

CASSIO
(*lifting his glass, with extreme excitement*)

My soul's an open book
And all may read it!

In fondo all'anima
Ciascun mi guardi!

(*He drinks.*)

I've nothing at all to hide...

Non temo il ver...

(*staggering*)

Nothing at all to hide...so be...

Non temo il ver... — e bevo...

ALL
(*laughing*)

Ah! Ah!   Ah! Ah!

CASSIO

The canakin   Del calice
Clinking...bubbles are winking at me...   Gli orli s'imporporino!...
(*He tries to repeat the first theme, but cannot remember the words.*)

IAGO
(*aside to Roderigo, while the others laugh at Cassio*)

(Now that he's drunk, we'll ruin him.   (Egli è ubriaco fradicio. Ti scuoti.
Approach him
And provoke him to quarrel; he'll lose his   Lo trascina a contesa; è pronto all'ira,
    temper,
He'll try to fight and it will cause a riot!   T'offenderà...ne seguirà tumulto!
That is the way to rouse our good Otello   Pensa che puoi così del lieto Otello
And end his bliss on his first night of love!)   Turbar la prima vigilia d'amore!)

RODERIGO
(*resolutely*)

(For that reason I'll do it.)   (Ed è ciò che mi spinge.)

MONTANO
(*entering and addressing Cassio*)

Captain Cassio,   Capitano,
The guard awaits your orders on the   V'attende la fazione ai baluardi.
    ramparts.

CASSIO
(*staggering*)

Let's go then!   Andiam!

40

MONTANO

What's this now?   Che vedo?

IAGO
(*to Montano*)

(Ev'ry night in the same way   (Ogni notte in tal guisa
Cassio prepares for duty.   Cassio preludia al sonno.

MONTANO

Otello should know it.)   Otello il sappia.)

CASSIO
(*as above*)

Let's go to the ramparts ...   Andiamo ai baluardi ...

RODERIGO, THEN ALL

Ah! Ah!   Ah! Ah!

CASSIO

Who's laughing?   Chi ride?

RODERIGO
(*provoking him*)

Look at the drunkard ...   Rido d'un ebro ...

CASSIO
(*hurling himself at Roderigo*)

Watch what you are saying!   Bada alle tue spalle!
You villain!   Furfante!

RODERIGO
(*defending himself*)

A knave and a drunkard!   Briaco ribaldo!

CASSIO

You scoundrel   Marrano!
For that I shall kill you!   Nessun più ti salva!

MONTANO
(*separating them by force and turning to Cassio*)

Control your behaviour,   Frenate la mano,
Good sir, I command you.   Signor, ve ne prego.

CASSIO
(*to Montano*)

I'll beat your brains out   Ti spacco il cerèbro
If you try to stop me.   Se qui t'interponi.

MONTANO

The words of a drunkard ...   Parole d'un ebro ...

CASSIO

A drunkard?   D'un ebro?!
(*Cassio draws his sword. Montano also arms himself. A violent fight ensues. The crowd retreats.*)

IAGO
(*aside to Roderigo, rapidly*)

(Roderigo, as fast as you can through   (Va al porto, con quanta più possa
The harbour go shouting: rebellion!   Ti resta, gridando: sommossa! sommossa!
rebellion!
Go! Cry it all over the town; get the   Va! spargi il tumulto, l'orror. Le campane
watchman
To sound the alarm.)   Risuonino a stormo.)

(*Roderigo runs out. Iago calls to the combatants, loudly.*)

My comrades! Have done with   Fratelli! l'immane
This barbarous duel!   Conflitto cessate!

WOMEN FROM THE CHORUS
(*fleeing*)

Away!   Fuggiam!

IAGO

What! Already   Ciel! già gronda
Montano is bleeding. A murderous quarrel!   Di sangue Montano! Tenzon furibonda!

CHORUS (OTHER WOMEN)

Away!   Fuggiam!

IAGO

Stop them! / Tregua!

ALL

Stop them! / Tregua!

WOMEN
(*fleeing*)

They'll kill themselves! / S'uccidono!

MEN
(*to the duellists*)

Stop them! / Pace!

IAGO
(*to the onlookers*)

Too late to restrain their impetuous fury! / Nessuno più raffrena quell'ira pugnace!
Go sound the alarm! They're seized by the devil! / Si gridi l'allarme! Satàna li invade!!

VOICES
(*on stage and off*)

The alarm bell!! / All'armi!!

(*Alarm bells are heard.*)

ALL

A rescue! / Soccorso!!

Scene Two. *Otello, Iago, Cassio, Montano, townspeople, soldiers, and later, Desdemona.*

OTELLO
(*followed by people carrying torches*)

Your blades cast before me! / Abbasso le spade!

(*The duellists drop their swords. Montano leans on a soldier. The clouds clear away gradually.*)

What's this! What happened! Am I among barbarians? / Olà! Che avvien? son io fra i Saraceni?
Or have you all been seized by Turkish fury / O la turchesca rabbia è in voi trasfusa
That you fight one another?...My honest Iago, / Da sbranarvi l'un l'altro?...Onesto Jago,
Now by your love for me, I charge you, tell me. / Per quell'amor che tu mi porti, parla.

IAGO

Who knows?...One moment we were all good companions, / Non so...qui tutti eran cortesi amici,
Friendly, and merry...on a sudden, just as / Dianzi, e giocondi...ma ad un tratto, come
If some star bringing evil passed overhead and / Se un pianeta maligno avesse a quelli
Bewitched their senses, they drew their weapons / Smagato il senno, sguainando l'arme
And fell on one another...And I would rather / S'avventano furenti...avess'io prima
Have lost a leg than be a witness! / Stroncati i pie' che qui m'addusser!

OTELLO

Cassio, / Cassio,
What has made you forgetful of duty?... / Come obliasti te stesso a tal segno?...

CASSIO

Pardon...Forgive...I know not how... / Grazia...perdon...parlar non so...

OTELLO

Montano... / Montano...

MONTANO
(*supported by a soldier*)

I am wounded... / Io son ferito...

OTELLO

You're wounded, by heaven. / Ferito!...pel cielo
My blood begins to boil! My guardian angel / Già il sangue mio ribolle. Ah! l'ira volge
Flies in dismay and leaves me filled with anger! / L'angelo nostro tutelare in fuga!

42

(Enter Desdemona. Otello rushes towards her.)

Ah! And my lovely Desdemona is roused from	Che? … la mia dolce Desdemona anch'essa
Her dreams, disturbed by vulgar riot. Cassio,	Per voi distolta da' suoi sogni?—Cassio,
You're my captain no longer.	Non sei più capitano.

(Cassio drops his sword which Iago recovers.)

IAGO
(handing Cassio's sword to an officer)

(And so I triumph!)	(Oh, mio trionfo!)

OTELLO

Iago, go lead the men of Cassio's squadron,	Jago, tu va nella città sgomenta
Patrol the town until the streets are safe.	Con quella squadra a ricompor la pace.

(Exit Iago.)

Take good care of Montano.	Si soccorra Montano.

(Montano is helped inside the castle.)

Let all return to	Al proprio tetto
Their own abodes.	Ritorni ognun.

(to all, imperiously)

I myself shall remain here	Io da qui non mi parto
Until the place is deserted around me.	Se pria non vedo deserti gli spalti.

Gradually the stage empties. Otello makes a sign to his torch-bearers to return to the castle.
Scene Three. *Otello and Desdemona.*

OTELLO

Now in the silent darkness	[6]	Già nella notte densa
The strife is heard no more.		S'estingue ogni clamor.
Now my heart that was raging		Già il mio cor fremebondo
Is lulled in sweetest calm as I embrace you.		S'ammansa in quest'amplesso e si rinsensa.
Thunder and war may crack all the world asunder		Tuoni la guerra e s'inabissi il mondo
When after boundless anger		Se dopo l'ira immensa
Comes such a boundless love!		Vien quest'immenso amor!

DESDEMONA

O my warrior so proud! So many torments	Mio superbo guerrier! quanti tormenti,
And such sad tender sighing, so many hopes	Quanti mesti sospiri e quanta speme
Have led our true loving hearts to these embraces!	Ci condusse ai soavi abbracciamenti!
Oh! It is sweet our murmuring together:	Oh! com'è dolce il mormorare insieme:
Do you remember!	Te ne rammenti!
Once when you told me of your life in exile,	Quando narravi l'esule tua vita
Of your adventures and your years of woe,	E i fieri eventi e i lunghi tuoi dolor,
And I was seized with rapture as I heard you,	Ed io t'udia coll'anima rapita
I shared those sorrows, my heart began to glow.	In quei spaventi e coll'estasi in cor.

OTELLO

I told of famous victories, of battles	Pingea dell'armi il fremito, la pugna
When we determined to conquer or die,	E il vol gagliardo alla breccia mortal,
Bold sorties, and climbing battlements, and trying to	L'assalto, orribil edera, coll'ugna
Scale the ramparts, while arrows whistled by.	Al baluardo e il sibilante stral.

DESDEMONA

Then you would lead me far beyond the ocean,	Poi mi guidavi ai fulgidi deserti,
Back to your homeland, that waste of burning sand,	All'arse arene, al tuo materno suol;
When you described that shameful fate you suffered,	Narravi allor gli spasimi sofferti
Sold into slavery, chained by a cruel hand.	E le catene e dello schiavo il duol.

OTELLO

But when you sighed so tenderly that suffering	Ingentilia di lagrime la storia

43

Became my glory. My sorrows then were light;
For on my sombre history you poured
A starry radiance, and made my darkness bright.

Il tuo bel viso e il labbro di sospir;
Scendean sulle mie tenebre la gloria,
Il paradiso e gli astri a benedir.

DESDEMONA

And I saw gleaming on your dusky forehead
All of the splendour that shines in your soul.

Ed io vedea fra le tue tempie oscure
Splender del genio l'eterea beltà.

OTELLO

Ah, how you loved me for those woes [7]
I'd suffered,
And how I loved you for your grief and care.

E tu m'amavi per le mie sventure
Ed io t'amavo per la tua pietà.

DESDEMONA

Ah, then I loved you for those woes you'd suffered,
And how you loved me for my grief and care.

Ed io t'amavo per le tue sventure
E tu m'amavi per la mia pietà.

OTELLO

Death you may claim me! Let me die in the ecstasy
Of this enchantment,
This moment of rapture!

Venga la morte! e mi colga nell'estasi
Di questo amplesso
Il momento supremo!

(*The night sky is by now completely clear. A few stars are visible, on the rim of the horizon the sky-blue reflection of the rising moon.*)

So sublime is my happiness I'm fearful
That I shall never more be granted…
Be granted such a moment
In the dark hidden years that lie before me.[11]

Tale è il gaudio dell'anima che temo,
Temo che più non mi sarà concesso
Quest'attimo divino
Nell'ignoto avvenir del mio destino.

DESDEMONA

Let heaven dispel your sorrows,
Our loving hearts will never be divided.

Disperda il ciel gli affanni
E Amor non muti col mutar degli anni.

OTELLO

I pray that heaven hears you,
"Amen" should answer from those spheres above me.

A questa tua preghiera
"Amen" risponda la celeste schiera.

DESDEMONA

"Amen" they answer.

"Amen" risponda.

OTELLO
(*leaning on the rampart*)

Ah! This joy that invades me [8]
So deeply that breathless, I tremble.
I kiss you…

Ah! la gioia m'innonda
Si fieramente… che ansante mi giacio.
Un bacio…

DESDEMONA

Otello!…

Otello!…

OTELLO

I kiss you… once more I kiss you.

Un bacio… ancora un bacio.

(*standing up and staring at the starry heavens*)

Now the stars of the Plough have met the ocean.

Già la pleiade ardente al mar discende.

DESDEMONA

Ah! It is late.

Tarda è la notte.

OTELLO

Come… Venus invites us!

Vien… Venere splende.

(*They make their way, arms around each other, towards the castle.*)

Curtain.

Act Two

Introduction [9a]/ *A ground-floor room in the castle. Through a window a large garden is seen. A balcony.* **Scene One.** *Iago on this side of the balcony. Cassio on the garden side.*

IAGO

Don't give up hope. But trust in me, and soon,	Non ti crucciar. Se credi a me, tra poco
We shall see you return to win the flighty favours	Farai ritorno ai folleggianti amori
Of Mistress Bianca, once more a dashing captain,	Di monna Bianca, altero capitano,
Wearing your sword with golden hilt beside you.	Coll'elsa d'oro e col balteo fregiato.

CASSIO

Do not deceive me...	Non lusingarmi...

IAGO

Attend to what I tell you.	Attendi a ciò ch'io dico.
Surely you know that Desdemona commands our	Tu dêi saper che Desdemona è il Duce
Noble commander, she's the sun he lives by.	Del nostro Duce, sol per essa ei vive.
All you must do is beg that gen'rous lady	Pregala tu, quell'anima cortese
To plead for Cassio then you will soon be pardoned.	Per te interceda e il tuo perdono è certo.

CASSIO

But how can I approach her?	Ma come favellarle?

IAGO

It is her wont to	È suo costume
Walk ev'ry afternoon under that arbor	Girsene a meriggiar fra quelle fronde
With my good wife Emilia. So there await her.	Colla consorte mia. Quivi l'aspetta
Now I've shown you the path to your own salvation,	Or t'è aperta la via di salvazione;
Take it.	Vanne.

Cassio moves away. **Scene Two.** *Iago alone.*

IAGO

(gazing after Cassio)

Take it; take the path to your ruin. [9]	Vanne; la tua meta già vedo.
Your evil genius drives you, your evil genius is Iago,	Ti spinge il tuo dimone, E il tuo dimon son io,
And I'm impelled by mine, that ruthless cruel	E me trascina il mio, nel quale io credo
Angry God I believe in.	Inesorato Iddio.

(moving away from the balcony, no longer looking at Cassio, who disappears through the trees)

Yes, I believe in God who has created [10]	— Credo in un Dio crudel che m'ha creato
Me like himself, cruel and vile he made me.	Simile a sé, e che nell'ira io nomo.
Born from some spawn of nature or from an atom,	— Dalla viltà d'un germe o d'un atòmo
Born into vileness.	Vile son nato.
So I am evil	— Sono scellerato
Because I'm human,	Perché son uomo,
Primeval slime has left its vileness in me.	E sento il fango originario in me.
Yes! This is Iago's creed!	Sì! quest'è la mia fe'!
Truly I do believe, just as the credulous	— Credo con fermo cuor, siccome crede
Widow in church believes in God,	La vedovella al tempio,
That all the evil that I do is destined,	— Che il mal ch'io penso e che da me procede
Fate alone directs me.	Per mio destino adempio.
Man says he's honest, he is a fool and liar	— Credo che il giusto è un istrìon beffardo
In his face and his heart;	E nel viso e nel cuor,
And all he does is falsehood:	Che tutto è in lui bugiardo:

45

Charity, kindness, kissing,	Lagrima, bacio, sguardo,
And the lies told by love.	Sacrificio ed onor.
Yes, I believe man is the fool of fortune;	— E credo l'uom gioco d'iniqua sorte
The cradle holds an infant	Dal germe della culla
Who's born to feed the worm.	Al verme dell'avel.
Then after life has run its course, Death. 11]	— Vien dopo tanta irrisîon la Morte.
And then? And then there's nothing.	— E poi?—La Morte è il Nulla.
And heaven's a foolish tale.	È vecchia fola il Ciel.

(Desdemona is seen walking in the garden with Emilia. Iago rushes to the balcony, beyond which Cassio waits.)

IAGO
(to Cassio)

There she is … Cassio … your chance …	Eccola … Cassio … a te … Questo è
And now's the moment.	il momento.
So hurry … there's Desdemona.	Ti scuoti … vien Desdemona.

(Cassio approaches Desdemona, greets her and walks beside her.)

She sees him, and he greets her	S'è mosso; la saluta
As he approaches.	E s'avvicina.
And now I need Otello! O Satan, come to	Or qui si tragga Otello! … aiuta, aiuta
Help me, Satan, come to help me!	Sàtana il mio cimento! …

(He remains on the balcony, looking out, but half-hidden. Cassio and Desdemona again come into view strolling in the garden.)

They are talking together … and she inclines her	Già conversano insieme … ed essa inclina,
Head and sweetly smiles upon him.	Sorridendo, il bel viso.
What pretty glances; one alone would serve me,	Mi basta un lampo sol di quel sorriso
One smile would break Otello's heart for ever.	Per trascinare Otello alla ruina.
To work …	Andiam …

(He is about to leave when he stops suddenly.)

But now I see that Fate is with me.	Ma il caso in mio favor s'adopra.
Here he is … I'm ready, I've caught him.	Eccolo … al posto all'opra.

He remains on the left side of the balcony, gazing fixedly at Cassio and Desdemona in the garden. **Scene Three.** *Iago and Otello.*

IAGO
(pretending not to have seen Otello approaching, and seeming to talk to himself)

How distressing …	Ciò m'accora …

OTELLO

What is it?	Che parli?

IAGO

Nothing … you here? Just an idle	Nulla … voi qui? una vana
Comment that had no meaning …	Voce m'usci dal labbro …

OTELLO

That man out there who from my	Colui che s'allontana
Wife is departing, is it Cassio?	Dalla mia sposa, è Casio?

(Both move away from the balcony.)

IAGO

Cassio? No … why should Cassio	Casio? no … quei si scosse
Sneak away when he sees you?	Come un reo nel vedervi.

OTELLO

Yet I am sure it's Cassio.	Credo che Cassio ei fosse.

IAGO

My good master …	Mio signore …

OTELLO

What is it?	Che brami? …

IAGO

Cassio, in those first days	Cassio, nei primi dì

46

When you were in love, was Cassio a friend of Desdemona?

Del vostro amor, Desdemona non conosceva?

OTELLO

Yes.

Si.

But why ask such a question?

Perché fai una tale inchiesta?

IAGO

I ask it out of vague Apprehension, not out of malice.

Il mio pensiero è vago D'ubbie, non di malizia.

OTELLO

Say what you're thinking, Iago.

Di'il tuo pensiero, Iago.

IAGO

And did you trust this Cassio?

Vi confidaste a Cassio?

OTELLO

Often he bore a token of Love to my Desdemona.

Spesso un mio dono o un cenno Portava alla mia sposa.

IAGO

He did so?

Dassenno?

OTELLO

Yes, he did so.
(*calmly*)
Is he not honest?

Si, dassenno.

Nol credi onesto?

IAGO
(*imitating Otello*)

Honest?

Onesto?

OTELLO

Come tell me what you're thinking?

Che ascondi nel tuo cuore?

IAGO

But what should I be thinking?

Che ascondo in cor, signore?

OTELLO

"But what should I be thinking?"
By heaven! you're the echo of all I say; I know in
That mind of yours you're hiding dark and atrocious secrets.
Yes; for I heard those muttered words you spoke: "How distressing".
Tell me what distressed you? When I said Cassio you wrinkled
Up your brow and denied it. Then speak, speak if you love me.

"Che ascondo in cor, signore?"
Pel cielo! tu sei l'eco dei detti miei;nel chiostro
Dell'anima ricetti qualche terribil mostro.
Si, ben t'udii poc'anzi mormorar "ciò m'accora".
Ma di che t'accoravi? nomini Cassio e allora
Tu corrughi la fronte. Suvvia, parla se m'ami.

IAGO

Well you know that I love you.

Voi sapete ch'io v'amo.

OTELLO

Then enough of concealment;
Tell me what you are thinking. You can speak to me freely.
Do not be tempted to spare me, tell me the worst that can happen!

Dunque senza velami
T'esprimi e senza ambagi. T'esca fuor dalla gola
Il tuo più rio pensiero colla più ria parola!

IAGO

Even though you should kill me, held my life in your fingers,
I'd be silent.

S'anco teneste in mano tutta l'anima mia

Nol sapreste.

OTELLO

Ah!

Ah!

IAGO
(*moving close to Otello, sottovoce*)

Beware, O my lord, lest jealousy seize you!
Fear that blind monster, jealousy, [12] jealousy, feeding on poison,
Whose taste is fatal, tearing a wound in your soul that never heals.

Temete, signor, la gelosia!
È un idra fosca, livida, cieca, col suo veleno
Sé stessa attosca, vivida piaga le squarcia il seno.

OTELLO

O God in heaven!! No! She first must give me cause for suspicion.	Misera mia!!—No, il vano sospettar nulla giova.
Before I doubt her I'll question her; if I doubt her I'll prove it;	Pria del dubbio l'indagine, dopo il dubbio la prova,
And if I prove it (Otello turns thoughts into action),	Dopo la prova (Otello ha sue leggi supreme)
Then jealousy and love will be destroyed together.	Amore e gelosia vadan dispersi insieme!

IAGO
(*growing bolder*)

Those ardent words unseal my lips and now I'll speak freely.	Un tal proposto spezza di mie labbra il suggello.
I do not talk of proof yet; but O my noble Otello,	Non parlo ancor di prova; pur, generoso Otello,
Just observe her, for often a free and trusting nature	Vigilate; soventi le oneste e ben create
Can overlook the signs that tell of falsehood: observe her.	Coscienze non sospettano la frode: vigilate.
And mark the sense of ev'ry word she says to you; one sentence	Scrutate le parole di Desdemona, un detto
Maybe will show she's guiltless, or confirm your suspicion.	Può ricondur la fede, può affermar il sospetto...
There she is; now observe her ...	Eccola; vigilate ...

(*Desdemona reappears in the garden, seen through the large opening downstage. She is surrounded by the island women, children and Cypriot and Albanian sailors, who come forward and present her with flowers and other gifts. Some accompany their singing on the guzla, others on small harps.*)

CHORUS
(*in the garden*)

At your glances flame in our	[13] Dove guardi splendono
Hearts leaps up to meet you,	Raggi, avvampan cuori;
Round your footsteps carpets of	Dove passi scendono
Flow'rs spring up to greet you.	Nuvole di fiori.
Here mid rose and lily,	Qui fra gigli e rose
As at sacred altars	Come a un casto altar
Fathers, children, maidens	Padri, bimbi, spose
Join to sing your praise.	Vengono a cantar.

CHILDREN
(*scattering lily petals on the ground*)

We bring you lilies	T'offriamo il giglio,
On slender stem ...	Soave stel
The flow'rs that angels love	Che in man degli angeli
To bear on high,	Fu assunto in ciel,
To lay on the hem of the	Che abbella il fulgido
Glorious mantle	Manto e la gonna
Of our Madonna	Della Madonna
Who dwells on high.	E il santo vel.

WOMEN AND SAILORS

As our song goes winging	Mentre all'aura vola
Rising up on high,	Lieta la canzon
Mandoline is strumming	L'agile mandòla
And guitars reply.	Ne accompagna il suon.

SAILORS
(*offering Desdemona coral and pearl necklaces*)

For you these coral gems,	A te le porpore,
From depths of ocean,	Le perle e gli ostri,
Jewels found beneath the waves,	Nella voragine
Pearls of softest shine.	Còlti del mar.
We'd adorn Desdemona	Vogliam Desdemona
With our richest treasures,	Coi doni nostri
Like some fair statue	Come un'immagine
In a holy shrine.	Sacra adornar.

As the song is winging	Mentre all'aura vola
Lightly, winging lightly,	Lieta la canzon,
Mandoline is strumming,	L'agile mandòla
And gay guitars reply.	Ne accompagna il suon.

WOMEN
(strewing fronds and flowers)

For you we gather'd flow'rs	A te la florida
All that the land bears,	Messe dei grembi
Clouds of fragrance,	A nembi, a nembi
In fragrant show'rs.	Spargiamo al suol.
The spring surrounds you,	L'April circonda
O bride of springtime	La sposa bionda
With radiant golden shine	D'un'etra rorida
Reflecting the sun's bright ray.	Che vibra al sol.

CHILDREN AND SAILORS

As the song is winging	Mentre all'aura vola
Lightly, winging lightly	Lieta la canzon
Mandoline is strumming,	L'agile mandòla
And gay guitars reply.	Ne accompagna il suon.

ALL

At your glances flame in our	Dove guardi splendono
Hearts leaps up to meet you,	Raggi, avvampan cuori;
Round your footsteps carpets	Dove passi scendono
Of flow'rs spring up to greet you.	Nuvole di fiori.
Here mid rose and lily,	Qui fra gigli e rose,
As at sacred altars	Come a un casto altar
Fathers, children, maidens	Padri, bimbi, spose
Join to sing your praise.	Vengono a cantar.

DESDEMONA

Heav'n is smiling,	Splende il cielo, danza
Breezes dance and flow'rs are sweet.	L'aura, olezza il fior.
Joy and hope conspire,	Gioia, amor, speranza
Smiling their song of hope.	Cantan nel mio cor.

CHORUS

Heaven will bless your love, will bless your love.	Vivi felice! Addio. Qui regna Amore.

(During the Chorus Otello looks on with Iago.)

OTELLO
(tenderly)

...Ah, how this song o'erwhelms me	...Quel canto mi conquide.
If she is guilty, then heav'n itself deceives me!	No, no, s'ella m'inganna, il ciel sé stesso irride!

IAGO

(So love and beauty are joined in sweet concord!	(Beltà ed amor in dolce inno concordi!
But soon I shall destroy their tender concord.)	I vostri infrangerò soavi accordi.)

Scene Four. *When the Chorus have finished, Desdemona kisses several children on the brow, and some of the women kiss the hem of her dress. She hands a purse to the sailors. The Chorus move away. Desdemona, with Emilia in attendance, enters the room and goes towards Otello.*

DESDEMONA
(to Otello)

I come from someone who has felt your anger [14]	D'un uom che geme sotto il tuo disdegno
And for him I am pleading.	La preghiera ti porto.

OTELLO

Who can that be?		Chi è costui?

DESDEMONA

Cassio.	Cassio.

Was it he / I saw beside you underneath that arbor?

Era lui / Che ti parlava sotto quelle fronde?

DESDEMONA

Yes, Cassio. And by his grief I'm moved so deeply;
He is repentant, he deserves forgiveness.
I am pleading for him; for him I implore you.
So please forgive him.

Lui stesso, e il suo dolor che in me s'infonde
Tant'è verace che di grazia è degno.
Intercedo per lui, per lui ti prego.
Tu gli perdona.

OTELLO

Not now.

Non ora.

DESDEMONA

O my lord, can you refuse me?
Please forgive him.

Non oppormi il tuo diniego.
Gli perdona.

OTELLO

Not now.

Non ora.

DESDEMONA

I can hear you are troubled,
Your voice is angry. What pain has come to hurt you?

Perché torbida suona
La tua voce? Qual pena t'addolora?

OTELLO

Here on my forehead ...

M'ardon le tempie ...

DESDEMONA

(*unfolding her handkerchief as if about to wipe Otello's forehead*)

All that ugly pain will
Quickly pass at the soothing
Touch of this linen when I bind your forehead.

Quell'ardor molesto
Svanirà, se con questo
Morbido lino la mia man ti fascia.

OTELLO

(*throwing the handkerchief to the ground*)

I've no need of your help.

Non ho d'uopo di ciò.

DESDEMONA

Ah, you are angry, My lord!

Tu sei crucciato, Signor!

OTELLO

(*harshly*)

O leave me!

Mi lascia!

(*Emilia picks up the handkerchief.*)

DESDEMONA

If unknowing I've done wrong, husband, forgive me.
Grant me, O grant me sweet words [15]
Of pardon, say you forgive me.
I am your gentle handmaid
Longing to help and serve you;
Ah, but I hear you sighing,
Why are your eyes cast down?
Look in my eyes and read there,
Read all my tender love.
For in my heart is comfort,
O let me ease your pain.

Se inconscia, contro te, sposo, ho peccato,
Dammi la dolce e lieta
Parola del perdono.
La tua fanciulla io sono
Umile e mansueta;
Ma il labbro tuo sospira,
Hai l'occhio fiso al suol.
Guardami in volto e mira
Come favella amore.
Vien, ch'io t'allieti il core,
Ch'io ti lenisca il duol.

IAGO

(*sottovoce to Emilia*)

Give me that kerchief
That you are holding.

Quel vel mi porgi
Ch'or hai raccolto.

EMILIA

(*sottovoce to Iago*)

Why do you want it?
What are you planning?

Qual frode scorgi?
Ti leggo in volto.

IAGO

Do not oppose me
When I command you.

T'opponi a vòto
Quand'io comando.

EMILIA

Yes I can see that / You plan some mischief.　　Il tuo nefando / Livor m'è noto.

IAGO

Your wild suspicions!　　Sospetto insano!

EMILIA

But I shall be / Her faithful guardian.　　Guardia fedel / È questa mano.

IAGO

Give it to me!　　Dammi quel vel!

(*He grasps Emilia's arm violently.*)

Obey or else you will / Feel my anger!　　Se te l'irosa / Mia man s'aggrava!

EMILIA

I am your wife, / I'm not your slave-girl.　　Son la tua sposa, / Non la tua schiava.

OTELLO

(*aside*)

(Maybe I lack the art of / Amusing conversation, / Maybe she finds me old and / Seeks a younger companion, / Maybe because my blackness / Alarms her tender soul, / O she is ruined and I am / Scorned, broken my heart / And ground to dust my longing, / Lost my dream of love.)

(Forse perché gli inganni / D'arguto amor non tendo, / Forse perché discendo / Nella valle degli anni, / Forse perché ho sul viso / Quest'atro tenebror, / Ella è perduta e irriso / Io sono e il cor m'infrango / E ruinar nel fango / Vedo il mio sogno d'ôr.)

IAGO

(You are the servant / And slave of Iago.　　(La schiava impura / Tu sei di Jago.

And in my heart I / Fear some misfortune.　　Ho il cor presago / D'una sventura.

Do you not fear me?　　Nè mi paventi?

EMILIA

You cruel man!　　Uomo crudel!

IAGO

Obey ...　　A me ...

EMILIA

　　　Why should I?　　　　　　　Che tenti?

IAGO

Obey! Obey!)　　A me quel vel!)

(*Iago snatches the handkerchief from Emilia.*)

(Now I have got what / I needed and Iago / Knows how to use it. / Yes I can use it!)　　(Già la mia brama / Conquido, ed ora / Su questa trama / Jago lavora!)

EMILIA

(I could not stop him / And he has snatched it. / God in your mercy / Guard her from danger.)　　(Vinser gli artigli / Truci e codardi. / Dio dai perigli / Sempre ci guardi.)

OTELLO

Now leave me! I must be alone.　　Escite! Solo vo' restar.

IAGO

(*sottovoce to Emilia who is about to leave*)

　　　　(And you must　　　　　　　(Ti giova
Be quiet. D'you hear me?)　　Tacer. Intendi?)

Exeunt Desdemona and Emilia. Iago also seems about to leave but reaching the door downstage, he stops. **Scene Five.** *Otello—Iago downstage.*

51

OTELLO
(in despair, seated on a chair)

Desdemona guilty!   Desdemona rea!

IAGO
(downstage, looking covertly at the handkerchief, then putting it carefully back inside his jerkin)

(This handkerchief can be my certain proof   (Con questi fili tramerò la prova
That she was false to her lord. Now I must   Del peccato d'amor. Nella dimora
  leave it
Where Cassio's sure to find it.)   Di Cassio ciò s'asconda.)

OTELLO

Can I believe it?   Atroce idea!

IAGO
(to himself, staring at Otello)

(I see my poison working.)   (Il mio velen lavora.)

OTELLO

Guilty to me! to me!!!   Rea contro me! contro me!!!

IAGO
(darkly)

(Cringe and suffer!)   (Soffri e ruggi!)

OTELLO

Betrayal!!! ... Betrayal!!! ...   Atroce!!! ... atroce!!!

IAGO
(good-humouredly, having moved to Otello's side)

Do not give it a thought!   Non pensateci più!

OTELLO
(jumping to his feet)

You? Beware me! Leave me!   Tu? Indietro! Fuggi!!
To the cross you have bound me! ...   M'hai legato alla croce! ...
Alas ... More dreadful than a crime   Ahimè ... Più orrendo d'ogni orrenda
  committed   ingiuria
Is the pain of suspicion.   Dell'ingiuria è il sospetto.
Those secret hours when she fed her passion   Nell'ore arcane della sua lussuria
(When I was cheated!) how could I suspect   (E a me furate!) m'agitava il petto
  them?
I had no reason. I was happy, oblivious ...   Forse un presagio? Ero baldo, giulivo ...
I could not guess the truth; I felt no treason   Nulla sapevo ancor; io non sentivo
In that fair lovely form, as I embraced her;   Sul suo corpo divin che m'innamora
Could not taste in her kisses   E sui labbri mendaci
The burning kisses   Gli ardenti baci
Of Cassio! But now! ... But now ...   Di Cassio! Ed ora! ... ed ora ...
Now and forever farewell all that I lived [16]   Ora è per sempre addio, sante memorie,
  for,
Farewell sublime enchantment of the mind!   Addio, sublimi incanti del pensier!
Farewell glittering arms, farewell my   Addio, schiere fulgenti, addio, vittorie,
  victories,
Gallant adventures on my cantering steed!   Dardi volanti e volanti corsier!
Farewell the banner that I bore in triumph!   Addio, vessillo trïonfale e pio,
When the peal of the trumpet called me to   E dïane squillanti in sul mattin!
  arms!
The call of clarion in the battle, farewell   Clamori e canti di battaglia, addio! ...
  now! ...
For Otello's glory's at an end.   Della gloria d'Otello è questo il fin.

IAGO

Calm now, my lord.   Pace, signor.

OTELLO

O you demon! Go find me   Sciagurato! mi trova
A visible token   Una prova secura
That Desdemona is guilty ...   Che Desdemona è impura ...
No escape! No escape! Nothing can help   Non sfuggir! non sfuggir! nulla ti
  you!   giova!
Find me a sure, visible, certain token!   Vo' una secura, una visibil prova!
Else I shall destroy you,   O sulla tua testa

52

A furious lightning flash will fall upon
Your head and my terrible anger will strike
  you!

S'accenda e precipiti il fulmine
Del mio spaventoso furor che si desta!

(grasping Iago by the throat and dragging him to the ground)

IAGO
(picking himself up)

The grace of heaven protect me now! May
  heaven
Protect you also. I'm no longer your ensign.
Now let me call upon the world to witness
How being true is rewarded.

Divina grazia, difendimi! Il cielo

Vi protegga. Non son più vostro alfiere.
Voglio che il mondo testimon mi sia
Che l'onestà è periglio.

(as if about to leave)

OTELLO
      No ... remain here.   No ... rimani.
For perhaps you are honest.   Forse onesto tu sei.

IAGO
(at the doorway, as if leaving)
          Better for me if   Meglio varrebbe
I'd supplied a lie.   Ch'io fossi un ciurmador.

OTELLO
       By all creation!   Per l'universo!
Can I believe in Desdemona? I do so
And yet I doubt her; you may be honest but
  maybe
You're a liar ... A proof is needed! Ah, I
Must be certain!!

Credo leale Desdemona e credo
Che non lo sia; te credo onesto e credo

Disleale ... La prova io voglio! voglio
La certezza!!

IAGO
(coming back to Otello)
   My lord, restrain your passion.   Signor, frenate l'ansie.
What proof could you accept as certain?
  Perhaps you
Would see them kissing?

E qual certezza v'abbisogna? Avvinti

Vederli forse?

OTELLO
    Ah! That would be a torment!!   Ah! Morte e dannazione!!

IAGO

And it wouldn't be easy; you cannot hope
  for
A certain proof, for how can deeds of
  darkness
Ever be seen by day? ... And yet there's
  something,
Something that may convince you,
  something that in itself
May seem but a trifle—not a proof but
Just a pointer t'wards the truth you seek.
  So hear it.

Ardua impresa sarebbe; e qual certezza

Sognate voi se quell'immondo fatto

Sempre vi sfuggirà? ... Ma pur se guida

È la ragione al vero, una si forte

Congettura riserbo che per poco
Alla certezza vi conduce. Udite:

(approaching close to Otello, sottovoce)

Darkness had fallen, Cassio was   [17]
  sleeping, I lay beside him.
With interrupted accents he uttered all he
  was thinking.
Softly he whispered, gently he murmured,
  telling his secrets
As he lay dreaming; clearly I heard him,
  all he was saying:
"Desdemona beloved! O let our love be
  secret.
We must be careful! Ah this sudden joy
  quite overwhelms me."
Then in his dreaming he moved towards
  me; with tender passion
Tried to embrace me as if he loved me, and
  then whispered:

Era la notte, Cassio dormìa, gli stavo
  accanto.
Con interrotte voci tradìa l'intimo incanto.

Le labbra lente, lente, movea, nell'
  abbandono
Del sogno ardente; e allor dicea, con flebil
  suono:
"Desdemona soave! Il nostro amor
  s'asconda.
Cauti vegliamo! L'estasi del ciel tutto
  m'innonda."
Seguìa più vago l'incubo blando; con molle
  angoscia,
L'interna imago quasi baciando, ei disse
  poscia:

"I curse the evil destiny that gave you to the Moor."
And then his dream passed. He feel into slumber, said no more.

"Il rio destino impreco che al Moro ti donò."
E allora il sogno in cieco letargo si mutò.

OTELLO

Now I am sure she's guilty!

Oh! mostruosa colpa!

IAGO

It was a dream I told you.

Io non narrai Che un sogno.

OTELLO

A dream can tell us what is true.

Un sogno che rivela un fatto.

IAGO

A dream sometimes confirms what we suspect for
Other reasons.

Un sogno che può dar forma di prova
Ad altro indizio.

OTELLO

What's that?

E qual?

IAGO

Do you remember
In Desdemona's hand a lovely kerchief
Adorned with flowers and, oh, so finely woven?

Talor vedeste
In mano di Desdemona un tessuto
Trapunto a fior e più sottil d'un velo?

OTELLO

That is the kerchief that I gave her, as my
First pledge of love.

È il fazzoletto ch'io le diedi, pegno
Primo d'amor.

IAGO

I saw that handkerchief yesterday
(Yes, I am sure) I saw it held by Cassio.

Quel fazzoletto ieri
(Certo ne son) lo vidi in man di Cassio.

OTELLO

Ah! Would that God had given him twenty thousand lives!
Ah! For then twenty thousand times I'd kill him!!
Iago, my heart is frozen.
And I renounce every form of pity.
All of my foolish love I change to hatred.
Look at me, beware me.
Crushed by the coils of the angry
Monster of jealousy! Ah! Blood! Blood! Blood!

Ah! mille vite gli donasse Iddio!
Una è povera preda al furor mio!!
Jago, ho il cuore di gelo.
Lungi de ma le pietose larve!
Tutto il mio vano amor esalo al cielo;
Guardami, ei sparve.
Nelle sue spire d'angue
L'idra m'avvince! Ah! sangue! sangue! sangue!

(He kneels.)

See me swear, you heav'ns above me! [18]
By the jagged lightning flash!
Hear me call, you angry sea below, fatal and dark!
I devote my soul to vengeance, soon the flame of hate will flash
From my hand as I now raise it!

Sì, per ciel marmoreo giuro! Per le attorte folgori!
Per la Morte e per l'oscuro mar sterminator!
D'ira e d'impeto tremendo presto fia che sfolgori
Questa man ch'io levo e stendo!

(He raises his hand to heaven. Otello is about to rise; Iago prevents him and kneels himself).

IAGO

Do not rise, my lord!
Hear me call the sun to witness, call that globe who lights my way,
Call the earth and all creation, hear my solemn vow!
To Otello I am faithful, heart and hand are his alone.
If he calls for deeds of vengeance gladly I obey!

Non v'alzate ancor!
Testimon è il Sol ch'io miro, che m'irradia e inanima,
L'ampia terra e il vasto spiro del Creato inter,
Che ad Otello io sacro ardenti, core, braccio ed anima
S'anco ad opere cruenti s'armi il suo voler!

IAGO AND OTELLO

(together, raising their hands to heaven, as if swearing a vow)

See me swear, you heav'ns above me! By the jagged lightning flash!
Hear me call, you angry sea below, fatal and dark!
I devote my soul to vengeance, soon the flame of hatred will
Fire this hand, this hand I raise now!

Sì, per ciel marmoreo giuro! per le attorte folgori!
Per la morte e per l'oscuro mar sterminator!
D'ira e d'impeto tremendo presto fia che sfolgori
Questa man ch'io levo e stendo. Dio vendicator!

Curtain.

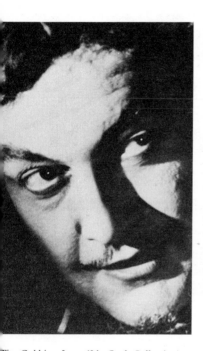

Tito Gobbi as Iago. (Ida Cook Collection)   *Helge Brilioth as Otello. (Covent Garden Archives)*

Act Three

The great hall of the castle. The stage is divided by a row of pillars around a large peristyle on the right. The characters can pass freely into the smaller room, adjoining the peristyle, which has a balcony at one end, upstage. **Scene One.** *Otello, Iago, the Herald.*

THE HERALD
(from the peristyle, to Otello who is in the room with Iago)

I bring word, that the watchman At the harbour has sighted the vessel of The envoys from Venice.	La vedetta del porto ha segnalato La veneta galea che a Cipro adduce Gli ambasciatori.

OTELLO
(to the Herald, motioning him to leave)

Make them welcome.	Bene sta.

(Exit the Herald.)

OTELLO
(to Iago)

Continue.	Continua.

IAGO

I've sent for Cassio and with my crafty questions	Qui trarrò Cassio e con astute inchieste
I'll lead him on to talk, while you in hiding	Lo adescherò a ciarlar. Voi là nascosto

(indicating the balcony)

Can hear his every word, observe his answers,	Scrutate i modi suoi, le sue parole,
His actions, his gestures. But control your anger	I lazzi, i gesti. Paziente siate
Or the proof will escape you. Here is Desdemona.	O la prova vi sfugge. Ecco Desdemona.
You must be careful ... I'll leave you.	Finger conviene ... io vado.

(He moves away as if to leave, then stops and approaches Otello again.)

Ask for the handerchief ...	Il fazzoletto ...

OTELLO

Go! Why remind me? I would gladly forget.	Va! volentieri obliato l'avrei.

Exit Iago. **Scene Two.** *Otello, Desdemona from the door on the left.*

DESDEMONA
(still by the doorway)

God give you joy, my husband, dear lord and ruler of my heart.	[19] Dio ti giocondi, o sposo dell'alma mia sovrano.

OTELLO
(going towards Desdemona and taking her hand)

Thank you, my lady, let me hold your snow-white hand in mine.	Grazie, madonna, datemi la vostra eburnea mano.
Warm is the dew that glows here upon this hand. *end cliff., indicates irony*	Caldo mador ne irrora la morbida beltà.

DESDEMONA

Ah, it has learned no sorrow, has felt not age or care.	Essa ancor l'orme ignora del duolo e dell'età.

OTELLO

And yet within this gentle hand there lurks a tiny devil.	Eppur qui annida il dèmone gentil del mal consiglio,
A crafty imp is hiding there, making this hand too gen'rous.	Che il vago avorio allumina del piccioletto artiglio.
To chastise him, fold your hands in repentance and holy fervour ...	Mollemente alla prece s'atteggia e al pio fervore ...

DESDEMONA

Recall my hand consented to give my heart to Otello.	Eppur con questa mano io v'ho donato il core.
But I have come to talk to you of Cassio.	Ma riparlar vi debbo di Cassio.

OTELLO

Again I feel that Burning pain in my forehead; will you help me to soothe it.	Ancor l'ambascia Del mio morbo m'assale; tu la fronte mi fascia.

56

DESDEMONA
(offering him a handkerchief)

Take this. · A te.

OTELLO

No; that handkerchief I gave you when first · No; il fazzoletto volgio ch'io ti donai.
we met.

DESDEMONA

It's not with me. · Non l'ho meco.

OTELLO

Desdemona, woe if you've lost it! Woe · Desdemona, guai se lo perdi! guai!
then!
For it was woven by an enchantress whose · Una possente maga ne ordia lo stame
powers were mighty: · arcano:
And while she wove it, she cast a spell · Ivi è risposta l'alta malia d'un talismano.
there, of dark enchantment.
Careful! To lose it, or give it away would · Bada! smarrirlo, oppur donarlo, è ria
bring disaster! · sventura!

DESDEMONA

Are you in earnest? · Il vero parli?

OTELLO

I am in earnest. · Il vero parlo.

DESDEMONA

Then heaven help me! ... · Mi fai paura! ...

OTELLO

What! Maybe you have lost it? · Che?! l'hai perduto forse?

DESDEMONA

No ... · No ...

OTELLO

Then fetch it. · Lo cerca.

DESDEMONA

I'll do so ... · Fra poco ...
I'll do so later ... · Lo cercherò ...

OTELLO

No, now! · No, tosto!

DESDEMONA

You are trying to tease me, [20] · Tu di me fai gioco.
Thus you reject my pleading for Cassio; · Storni cosi l'inchiesta di Cassio; astuzia
O sly Otello, · è questa
I see your plan. · Del tuo pensier.

OTELLO

By heaven! I feel my blood is boiling! · Pel cielo! l'anima mia si desta!
Go find that handkerchief ... · Il fazzoletto ...

DESDEMONA

To Cassio you've always been devoted. · È Cassio l'amico tuo diletto.

OTELLO

Go find that handkerchief!! · Il fazzoletto!!

DESDEMONA

Let Cassio be pardoned ... · A Cassio perdona ...

OTELLO

Go, find that handkerchief!! · Il fazzoletto!!

DESDEMONA

O God! I hear you threaten, your voice is · Gran Dio! nella tua voce v'è un grido di
dark with fury! · minaccia!

OTELLO

Raise up those glances! · Alza quegli occhi!
(seizing her by the neck and shoulders and forcing her to look at him)

DESDEMONA

A dreadful thought! · Atroce idea!

OTELLO

Look in my eyes! · Guardami in faccia!
Tell me, who are you? · Dimmi chi sei!

DESDEMONA

The true loving wife of Otello.　　　　　　　　La sposa fedel d'Otello.

OTELLO

　　　　Swear it!　　　　　　　　　　　　　　　　Giura!

Damn yourself swearing…　　　　Giura e ti danna…

DESDEMONA

Otello must know I'm honest.　　　　　　Otello fedel mi crede.

OTELLO

　　　I know you're　　　　　　　　　　　　Impura

Not honest.　　　　　　　　　　Ti credo.

DESDEMONA

Then heaven help me!　　　　　　Iddio m'aiuti!

OTELLO

　　Run to your own damnation,　　　　　　Corri alla tua condanna,

Swear you are faithful.　　　　　Di' che sei casta.

DESDEMONA

(staring at him)

Faithful I am…　　　　　　　　　　Casta… io son…

OTELLO

　　Swear it and damn yourself!!!　　　　　　　Giura e ti danna!!!

DESDEMONA

You glare at me in anger, I meet your　　Esterrefatta fisso lo sguardo tuo tremendo,
glance and fear it,

In you I hear a fury, I hear it, and I'm　　In te parla una Furia, la sento e non
bewildered.　　　　　　　　　　　　　l'intendo.

Behold me! Observe my eyes and read　　Mi guarda! Il volto e l'anima ti svelo; il
what's in them; my heart lies open　　　core infranto

Before you… I pray to heaven, for you　　Mi scruta… io prego il cielo per te con
these tears are falling,　　　　　　　　questo pianto.

For you this crystal stream of despairing　　Per te con queste stille cocenti aspergo il
and sorrow flows.　　　　　　　　　　suol.

See them, the first sad tears I shed; reply:　　Guarda le prime lagrime che da me spreme
Desdemona is true.　　　　　　　　　il duol.

OTELLO

If your demon could see you now, he'd　　S'or to scorge il tuo dèmone, un angelo
take you for an angel　　　　　　　　ti crede

And would reject you.　　　　　　E non t'afferra.

DESDEMONA

God sees my heart and knows me faithful!　　　Vede l'Eterno la mia fede!

OTELLO

No! It's Satan who sees you.　　　　No! La vede l'inferno.

DESDEMONA

　　　　For justice I implore you,　　　　　　La tua giustizia impetro,

O my husband!　　　　　　　Sposo mio!

OTELLO

Ah! Desdemona! Leave me! Yes, leave　　Ah! Desdemona!—Indietro! Indietro!
me! O leave me!　　　　　　　　　Indietro!

DESDEMONA

You are weeping?!… with a secret torment　　Tu pur piangi?!… e gemendo freni del
your heart is breaking!　　　　　　　cor lo schianto

Ah, can I be the cause of your grief, when I　　E son io l'innocente cagion di tanto pianto!
am blameless!

Have I offended?　　　　　　Qual è il mio fallo?

OTELLO

You ask me?… On your brow see it written,　　　　E il chiedi?… Il più nero delitto

On that white lovely brow in letters of　　Sovra il candido giglio della tua fronte è
flame it's written.　　　　　　　　scritto.

DESDEMONA

Alas!　　　　　　　Ahimè!

OTELLO

What! You deny you're a treacherous harlot?　　Che? non sei forse una vil cortigiana?

58

DESDEMONA

Ah! No! No! Let me swear it on my faith as a Christian!...	Ciel! No...no...pel battesmo della fede cristiana!...

OTELLO

What?	Che?

DESDEMONA

I am not, I swear it, that horrid word you called me.	Non son ciò che esprime quella parola orrenda.

(Changing suddenly from anger to a more frightening ironic calm, Otello takes Desdemona by the hand and leads her to the door by which she entered.) repeato theme from begin of duet

OTELLO

Then let me hold again that white hand; [19] I ask your pardon.	Datemi ancor l'eburnea mano, vo' fare ammenda.
I mistook you (please forgive me, I'm sorry I wronged you)	Vi credea (perdonate se il mio pensiero è fello)
For the vile filthy harlot who's the wife of Otello.	Quella vil cortigiana ch'è la sposa d'Otello.

With these words, Otello, who has now reached the door on the left, forces Desdemona out of the room with a brusque movement. He returns, in utter despair, to the centre of the stage.
Scene Three.

OTELLO

Heav'n! Had it pleased you to try me with affliction,	Dio! mi potevi scagliar tutti i mali
With bitter torment, shameful dishonour,	Della miseria,—della vergogna,
Change all my triumphs, my deeds of adventure	Far de' miei baldi trofei trionfali
Into a mockery, turn them to ashes...	Una maceria,—una menzogna...
I should have carried with patience that cross	E avrei portato la croce crudel
Of anguish and borne it	D'angosce e d'onte
With calm submission	Con calma fronte
And been resigned to the ordnance of [21] heaven.	E rassegnato al volere del ciel.
But, oh pain, oh grief! I have lost my fair vision	Ma, o pianto, o duol! m'han rapito il miraggio
By whose bewitchment I was enchanted.	Dov'io, giulivo,—l'anima acqueto.
All now is lost, all I lived for, the radiant	Spento è quel sol, quel sorriso, quel raggio
Star that inspired me, filling my soul with joy!	Che me fa vivo,—che mi fa lieto!
And tender Pity, you angel of grace	Tu alfin, Clemenza, pio genio immortal
Inspiring mercy,	Dal rosco riso,
Cover your gentle features,	Copri il tuo viso
Assume a grim aspect of hell!	Santo coll'orrida larva infernal!

Scene Four. *Otello, then Iago.*

OTELLO

Ah! Damned for ever!	Ah! Dannazione!
I will make her confess it and then I'll kill her!	Pria confessi il delitto e poscia muoia!
I must know! I must know!	Confession! Confessione...

(Enter Iago.)

I'll prove it!	La prova!...

IAGO

(beside Otello and pointing to the entrance)

Cassio's here!	Cassio è là!

OTELLO

Here? Great God!	Là?! Cielo! gioia!

(with a sudden shudder of horror)

But oh! What cruel torment!!	Orror!—Supplizi immondi!!

IAGO

Now hurry! Into hiding!	Ti frena! Ti nascondi.

59

He leads Otello quickly towards the balcony; he runs to the back of the peristyle where Cassio is standing, undecided whether to enter. **Scene Five.** *Otello (hidden), Iago and Cassio.*

IAGO

Come now; the hall's deserted.
So join me, my gallant captain.

Vieni; l'aula è deserta.
T'inoltra, o Capitano.

CASSIO

I'm a captain no more, I have been stripped
Of my rank.

Questo nome d'onor suona ancor vano
Per me.

IAGO

Take heart, for with her as your champion
Your victory is certain.

Fa cor, la tua causa è in tal mano
Che la vittoria è certa.

CASSIO

I thought that maybe I should find
Desdemona.

Io qui credea di ritrovar Desdemona.

OTELLO
(*hidden*)

(He spoke her name.)

(Ei la nomò.)

CASSIO

I want once more to see her
To discover if my pardon is granted.

Vorrei parlarle ancora,
Per saper se la mia grazia e profferta.

IAGO
(*gaily*)

Await her; and meanwhile I know that you must be
Eager to tell me all your new adventures:
What is the news of that poor girl who loves you?

L'attendi; e intanto, giacché non si stanca
Mai la tua lingua nelle fole gaie,
Narrami un po' di lei che t'innamora.

(*leading Cassio close to the first column of the peristyle*)

CASSIO

Which one?

Di chi?

IAGO
(*almost sottovoce*)

Why, Bianca!

Di Bianca!

OTELLO

(He's smiling!)

(Sorride!)

CASSIO

Folly!

Baie!...

IAGO

Are you a victim
Of her bright eyes?

Essa t'avvince
Coi vaghi rai.

CASSIO

You make me laugh.

Rider mi fai.

IAGO

Laughing is winning.

Ride chi vince.

CASSIO
(*laughing*)

Only too true in duels of love,
Laughing is winning. Ah! Ah!

In tal disfide,—per verità,
Vince chi ride, Ah! Ah!

IAGO

Ah! Ah!

Ah! Ah!

OTELLO
(*from the balcony*)

(He is triumphant, and his laughter will kill me,
God give me strength now to bear all my grief!)

(L'empio trionfa, il suo scherno m'uccide;
Dio, frena l'ansia che in core mi sta!)

CASSIO

And Bianca's kisses
Ah, how they bore me.

Son già di baci
Sazio e di lai.

60

IAGO

You make me laugh.   Rider mi fai.

CASSIO

Ah, love is fleeting!   O amor' fugaci!

IAGO

A new adventure captures your heart.   Vagheggi il regno—d'altra beltà.
Have I guessed it rightly?   Colgo nel segno?

CASSIO

                        Ah! Ah!   Ah! Ah!

IAGO

                        Ah! Ah!   Ah! Ah!

OTELLO

(He is triumphant, and his laughter will   (L'empio trionfa, il suo scherno m'uccide;
kill me;
God give me strength now to bear all my   Dio, frena l'ansia che in core mi sta!)
grief!)

CASSIO

You have guessed it rightly.   Nel segno hai côlto.
Yes, I confess it.   Si, lo confesso.
Listen...   M'odi...

IAGO
(*almost sottovoce*)

                Tell me your   Sommesso
Secret. I'm listening.   Parla. T'ascolto.

CASSIO
(*almost sottovoce, while Iago leads him to the part of the stage farthest away from Otello. Now and then words are distinguishable.*)

Iago, you know   Iago, t'e nota
That house where I'm staying...   La mia dimora...

. . . .

(*The words are lost.*)

OTELLO
(*cautiously, moving closer to hear what they are saying*)

(And now he's telling the manner,   (Or gli racconta il modo,
The place, the hour...)   Il luogo e l'ora...)

CASSIO
(*continuing to speak sottovoce*)

. . . .
And someone left there...   Da mano ignota...

. . . .

(*The words are lost.*)

OTELLO

(I can't hear what he's saying...   (Le parole non odo...
Closer! I must overhear! What have I come   Lasso! udir le vorrei! Dove son giunto!!)
to!!)

CASSIO

. . . .
A broidered kerchief...   Un vel trapunto...

. . . .

IAGO

She left it! How charming!   È strano! È strano!

OTELLO

(I must approach them, Iago gives the   (D'avvicinarmi Jago mi fa cenno.)
signal.)

(*Gradually, Otello, moving behind the columns with great caution, manages to draw close to the pair.*)

IAGO
(*sottovoce*)

While you were absent?   Da ignota mano?
                            (*loudly*)
Nonsense!   Baie!

61

CASSIO

Yes, truly.   Da senno.

(*Iago makes a sign to him to speak lower.*)

So I am eager   Quanto mi tarda
To learn who left it...   Saper chi sia...

IAGO

(*to himself, with a quick glance towards Otello*)

(Otello's watching.)   (Otello spia.)

(*loudly to Cassio*)

Then show it!   L'hai teco?

CASSIO

(*He draws Desdemona's handkerchief from his jerkin.*)

Here it is.   Guarda.

IAGO

(*taking the handkerchief*)

Ah how delightful!   Qual meraviglia!

(*aside*)

(Otello's listening.   (Otello origlia.
He's approaching   Ei s'avvicina
With stealthy footsteps.)   Con mosse accorte.)

(*bending with a laugh towards Cassio and putting his hands behind his back so that Otello can see the handkerchief*)

Who can resist you? Visiting angels   Bel cavaliere, nel vostro ostel
Leave both their virtue and their veils behind.   Perdono gli angeli—l'aureola e il vel.

OTELLO

(*drawing as close as he can to the handkerchief, behind Iago, hidden by the first column*)

(That's it. She gave it!   (È quello! è quello!
O mortal anguish!)   Ruina e Morte!)

IAGO

(Otello's listening.)   (Origlia Otello.)

OTELLO

(*hidden behind the column and from time to time looking at the handkerchief in Cassio's hands*)

(All is ended! Both love and grief!   (Tutto è spento! Amore e duol.
And my heart has turned to stone.   L'alma mia nessuna più smova.
She betrayed me, I have proved it;   Tradimento, la tua prova
Crimes of darkness shine by day.)   Spaventosa mostri al Sol.)

IAGO

(*to Cassio, pointing to the handkerchief*)

Love is a spider   [23] Quest'è una ragna
Cunning and wise,   Dove il tuo cuor
This is the cobweb,   Casca, si lagna,
And men are flies.   S'impiglia e muor.
If you admire it,   Troppo l'ammiri,
You must beware   Troppo la guardi;
When you desire it,   Bada ai deliri
You're in a snare.   Vani e bugiardi.
Love is a spider   Quest'è una ragna
Cunning and wise,   Dove il tuo cuor
This is the cobweb,   Casca, si lagna,
And men are flies.   S'impiglia e muor.

CASSIO

(*looking at the handkerchief which he has meantime retrieved from Iago*)

O fair shining marvel   Miracolo vago
What needle could make you,   Dell'aspo e dell'ago
You sparkle so brightly   Che in raggi tramuta
With rays from above,   Le fila d'un vel;
So whitely, so lightly,   Più bianco, più lieve
A delicate flake of snow,   Che fiocco di neve,
Of starry beams they wove you   Che nube tessuta
To fill men with love.   Dall'aure del ciel.

(*Trumpet fanfare off-stage, then a cannon shot. Otello has returned to the balcony.*)

62

IAGO

That is the signal to tell that the envoys
Coming from Venice have safely landed.
And listen.

Quest'è il segnale che annuncia l'approdo
Della trireme veneziana. Ascolta.

(fanfares from all sides)

All of the castle is ringing with trumpets.
If you remain here Otello will find you,
Off now.

Tutto il castel co' suoi squilli risponde.
Se qui non vuoi con Otello scontrarti,
Fuggi.

CASSIO

I'll leave you.

Addio.

IAGO

Go.

Va.

Exit Cassio quickly. **Scene Six.** *Iago and Otello.*

OTELLO

(moving closer to Iago)

How shall I take her life?

Come la ucciderò?

IAGO

And did you see how he was laughing?

Vedeste ben com'egli ha riso?

OTELLO

I saw it.

Vidi.

(Intermittent fanfares and shouts of joy are heard.)

IAGO

You saw the kerchief?

E il fazzoletto?

OTELLO

I saw ev'rything.

Tutto vidi.

VOICES

(off-stage, distant)

Evviva!
To the harbour! They are landing!

Evviva!
Alla riva! Allo sbarco!

OTELLO

And it condemns her.
Go prepare me a draught of deadly poison.

È condannata.
Fa ch'io m'abbia un velen per questa notte.

VOICES

(nearer)

Evviva! Evviva! The Lion of St Mark!

Evviva! Evviva! il Leon di San Marco!

IAGO

Not poison, no. Your best way is to choke her,
There in her bed, there where she betrayed you.

Il tosco no, val meglio soffocarla,
Là nel suo letto, là, dove ha peccato.

OTELLO

Yes, I approve your plan, that's fitting.

Questa giustizia tua mi piace.

IAGO

With Cassio,
Iago himself will deal.

A Cassio
Jago provvederà.

OTELLO

Iago, from this day
Forth I appoint you my captain.

Jago, fin d'ora
Mio capitano t'eleggo.

IAGO

My noble
Lord, I thank you.

Mio Duce,
Grazie vi rendo.

(The noises grow louder. Fanfares and shouts.)

Envoys have come from Venice.
You must meet them. But to avoid suspicion
Desdemona should be with you to greet them.

Ecco gli ambasciatori.
Li accogliete. Ma ad evitar sospetti,
Desdemona si mostri a quei Messeri.

OTELLO

Yes, go to call her.

Sì, qui l'adduci.

Exit Iago by the door on the left; Otello goes to receive the envoys. **Scene Seven.** *Otello, Lodovico, Roderigo, the Herald, Dignitaries of the Venetian Republic, Gentlemen and*

Ladies, Soldiers, Trumpeters upstage; then Iago with Desdemona and Emilia, from the left.
(The Ballet written for the Paris première was inserted here.)

LODOVICO
(holding a rolled-up parchment in his hand)

The Doge and all the Senate	Il Doge ed il Senato
Through me salute the all-victorious hero	Salutano l'eroe trionfatore
Of Cyprus. And as their envoy I have brought you	Di Cipro. Io reco nelle vostre mani
The decree of the Council.	Il messaggio dogale.

OTELLO
(accepting the missive and kissing the seal)

In humble duty	Io bacio il segno
I kiss the symbol of their might.	Della sovrana Maestà.

LODOVICO
(approaching Desdemona)

My lady,	Madonna,
May kind heav'n safely guard you.	V'abbia il cielo in sua guardia.

DESDEMONA

May heav'n hear you.	E il ciel v'ascolti.

EMILIA
(aside to Desdemona)

(Why all this sadness?	(Com sei mesta!

DESDEMONA
(aside to Emilia)

Emilia! Some evil shadows	Emilia! una gran nube
Cloud the mind of Otello and cloud My future.)	Turbe il senno d'Otello e il mio destino.)

IAGO
(approaching Lodovico)

Be welcome, Messere Lodovico.	Messer, son lieto di vedervi.

(Lodovico, Desdemona and Iago gather in a group.)

LODOVICO

Iago,	Iago,
What's the news here? And why is Cassio not Among you?	Quali nuove?... ma in mezzo a voi non trovo Cassio.

IAGO

With him Otello's angry.	Con lui crucciato è Otello.

DESDEMONA

I'm sure	Credo
He'll soon return to grace.	Che in grazia tornerà.

OTELLO
(to Desdemona, rapidly while pretending to read)

Are you so certain?	Ne sieta certa?

DESDEMONA

What say you?	Che dite?

LODOVICO

He's reading, did not hear you.	Ei legge, non vi parla.

IAGO

Perhaps	Forse
He'll soon return to grace.	Che in grazia tornerà.

DESDEMONA

Iago, I hope so;	Iago, lo spero;
All know how tenderly I feel toward our Cassio...	Sai se un verace affetto io porti a Cassio...

OTELLO
(still reading; feverishly sottovoce, to Desdemona)

Then keep your chattering tongue from its wagging...	Frenate dunque le labbra loquaci...

DESDEMONA

O forgive me, my lord...	Perdonate, signor...

OTELLO
(*hurling himself at Desdemona*)
You fiend, be silent!   Demonio, taci!!

LODOVICO
(*rushing to stay Otello's hand*)
No!   Ferma!

ALL
Oh horror!   Orrore!

LODOVICO
My mind will not believe what   La mente mia non osa
My eyes have had to witness.   Pensa ch'io vidi ilvera.

OTELLO
(*suddenly, and imperiously, to the Herald*)
Go call Cassio!   A me Cassio!

(*Exit the Herald.*)

IAGO
(*moving quickly to Otello's side, speaking in a low voice*)
(Why call him?)   (Che tenti?)

OTELLO
(*to Iago in a low voice*)
(Watch her when first he enters.)   (Guardala mentr'ei giunge.)

ALL
Unhappy lady!   Ah! triste sposa!

LODOVICO
(*in a low voice, drawing nearer to Iago, who has moved a short way away from Otello*)
And can that be the hero? That be the   Quest'è dunque l'eroe? quest'è il guerriero
soldier
You obey as your leader?   Dai sublimi ardimenti?

IAGO
(*to Lodovico, shrugging his shoulders*)
He's what he is.   È quel ch'egli è.

LODOVICO
Come tell me what you're thinking.   Palesa il tuo pensiero.

IAGO
Where he's concerned my tongue had best   Meglio è tener su ciò la lingua muta.
be silent.

Scene Eight. *Cassio, followed by the Herald, and the above.*

OTELLO
(*whose eyes never leave the door*)
(There he is! He's here!   (Eccolo! È lui!
(*moving towards Iago as Cassio is about to enter*)
Observe his ev'ry action.)   Nell'animo lo scruta.)
(*loudly for all to hear*)
All hear me! The Doge...   Messeri! il Doge...
(*harshly but sottovoce to Desdemona*)
(now pretend you're weeping)   — (ben tu fingi il pianto)
(*loudly for all to hear*)
Has recalled me to Venice.   Mi richiama a Venezia.

RODERIGO
(My hopes are shattered!)   (Infida sorte!)

OTELLO
(*continuing to speak loudly but in control of himself*)
And he's appointed   E in Cipro elegge
To take my place the man who served so   Mio successor colui che stava accanta
faithfully
Beside me, Cassio.   Al mio vessillo, Cassio.

IAGO
(*with vehemence and surprise*)
(Infernal torment!)   (Inferno e morte!)

OTELLO
(*continuing as above, he displays the parchment*)
Thus the Doge has decreed and I obey him.   La parola Ducale è nostra legge.

CASSIO
(kneeling to Otello)
And so shall I.   Obbedirò.

OTELLO
(quickly and covertly to Iago, pointing to Cassio)
(See him? The news is not to   (Vedi? non par che esulti
His liking.   L'infame?

IAGO
          No.)   No.)

OTELLO
(loudly for everyone to hear)
The men whom I commanded   La ciurma e la coorte
(speaking very rapidly and sottovoce to Desdemona)
(Continue with your whining...)   (Continua i tuoi singulti...)
(loudly for all to hear, no longer looking at Cassio)
And the fleet and the fortress   E le navi e il castello
I leave in charge of your new gen'ral.   Lascio in poter del nuovo Duce.

LODOVICO
(to Otello, pointing to Desdemona, who approaches as a suppliant)
                    Otello,   Otello,
Now be kind, comfort her, her heart is   Per pietà la conforta o il cor le infrangi.
  breaking.

OTELLO
(to Lodovico and Desdemona)
We shall embark at daybreak.   Noi salperem domani.
(In his fury, he seizes Desdemona.)
          So lie there! And weep there!   A terra!... e piangi!...

(Desdemona falls. Emilia and Lodovico run to her aid, raising her gently. Otello, in a fearsome rage, has thrown the parchment to the ground. Iago retrieves it and secretly reads it.)

DESDEMONA
I lie here! Yes... I lie in the   A terra!... sì... nel livido
Dust... rejected... I lie here   Fango... percossa... io giacio...
Grieving... some evil force has changed   Piango... m'agghiaccia il brivido
That noble heart I love.   Dell'anima che muor.
One day my life was smiling   [24]   E un dì sul mio sorriso
When love and hope inspired me,   Fioria la speme e il bacio
But now despair and anguish   Ed or... l'angoscia in viso
Close my husband's heart.   E l'agonia nel cor.
The sun whose splendour fills the sky   Quel sol sereno e vivido
Whose radiance cheers this calm shore   Che allieta il cielo e il mare
May shine on me but oh! his   Non può asciugar le amare
Beam will dry these tears no more.   Stille del mio dolor.

EMILIA
(No angry sign of hate she'll show,   (Quella innocente un fremito
Ah she is true and gentle;   D'odio non ha né un gesto,
Checks in her heart that cry of woe...   Trattiene in petto il gemito
Seeks to conceal her grief.   Con doloroso fren.
Her silent tears are falling,   La lagrima si frange
Pure drops of tender sorrow;   Muta sul volto mesto;
Who sees unmoved her suffering   No, chi per lei non piange
Must have a heart of stone.)   Non ha pietade in sen.)

RODERIGO
(My hopes are plunged in darkness,   (Per me s'oscura il mondo,
And cruel fate's unkind;   S'annuvola il destin;
She will depart at daybreak   L'angiol soave e biondo
And I am left behind.)   Scompar dal mio cammin.)

CASSIO
(My time has come! A lightning flash   (L'ora è fatal! un fulmine
Lights up the path before me.   Sul mio cammin l'addita.
Glory and fame await me here,   Già di mia sorte il culmine
All is within my grasp.   Soffre all'inerte man.
But can I trust my fortune   L'ebbra fortuna incalza

When storm is all around me.
Waves that can bear me upward
Can also bring me down.)

La fuga della vita.
Questa che al ciel m'innalza
È un'onda d'uragan.)

LODOVICO

(He raised his hand against her,
Blind rage and fury seize him;
She turns her face to heaven
Seeks for relief on high.
All behold her weeping
Weep in their hearts to see her,
All must weep. Her lamentation
Would melt a heart of stone.)

(Egli la man funerea
Scuote anelando d'ira,
Essa la faccia eterea
Volge piangendo al ciel.
Nel contemplar quel pianto
La carità sospira,
E un tenero compianto
Stempra del core il gel.)

(*The Chorus converse in groups.*)

WOMEN

Be kind!

Pietà!

MEN

Mysterious!

Mistero!

WOMEN

Terror and anguish, seize on
Their spirits, dark souls in torment and dismay.

Ansia mortale, bieca,
Ne ingombra, anime assorte in lungo orror.

MEN

Black are his features, black is his anger, by savage
Rage his soul is shaken, cruel and dark.

Quell'uomo nero è sepolcrale, e cieca
Un'ombra è in lui di morte e di terror.

WOMEN

O cruel sight!

Vista crudel!

MEN

With trembling fingers he claws his
Bosom! He gazes wildly at the ground.
Then lifts his eyes, his fist he clenches, as he
Defies the pow'rs above to strike him.

Strazie coll'ugna l'orrido
Petto! Figge gli sguardi immoti al suol.
Poi sfida il cielo coll'atre pugna, l'ispido
Aspetto ergendo ai dardi alti del Sol.

WOMEN

He struck his wife! Ah see those lovely, pure and tender
Features are stained with grief,
It's thus that angels weep with tears of holy grief
When some poor lost soul's condemn'd to die.

Ei la colpì! quel viso santo, pallido,
Blando, si china e tace e piange e muor.
Piangon così nel ciel lor pianto gli angeli
Quando perduto giace il peccator.

IAGO

(*approaching Otello who is slumped, in utter despair, in a chair*)

Let me advise you.

Una parola.

OTELLO

What then?

E che?

IAGO

Act quickly! Do not
Delay in taking your vengeance! The time is flying.

T'affretta! Rapido
Slancia la tua vendetta! Il tempo vola.

OTELLO

You're right.

Ben parli.

IAGO

And words alone are useless! Stir yourself!
Arouse yourself to action! Yes, think of action!
I'll deal with Cassio. He will rejoice no longer,
In hell he must atone for all his crime!

È l'ira inutil ciancia! Scuotiti!
All'opra ergi tua mira! All'opra sola!
Io penso a Cassio. Ei le sue trame espia.
L'infame anima ria l'averno inghiotte!

OTELLO

But who will kill him?   Chi gliela svelle?

IAGO

I.   Io.

OTELLO

You?   Tu?

IAGO

I swear.   Giurai.

OTELLO

So be it.   Tal sia.

IAGO

Tonight the news of Cassio's death will reach you.   Tu avrai le sue novelle in questa notte...

(*He leaves Otello and moves towards Roderigo, to whom he speaks ironically.*)

And so your love will sail away tomorrow   I sogni tuoi saranno in mar domani
And leave you on the quayside!   E tu sull'aspra terra!

RODERIGO
(*to Iago*)

I'm wretched!   Ahi, triste!

IAGO

You're foolish!   Ahi, stolto,
Foolish! You only have to hope. So stir   Stolto! Se vuoi, tu puoi sperar; gli umani,
Yourself and show some courage; now hear me.   Orsù! cimenti afferra, e m'odi.

RODERIGO

I'm listening.   Ascolto.

IAGO

Otello's ship will sail at daybreak, and Cassio's   Col primo albor salpa il vascello. Or Cassio
Ruler. But if some accident occurs to   È il Duce. Eppur se avvien che a questi accada

(*touching his sword*)

Our Cassio... Otello must remain here.   Sventura... allor qui resta Otello.

RODERIGO

How can I   Lùgubre
Make that accident sure?   Luce d'atro balen!

IAGO

Sword at the ready!   Mano all spada!
And when it's dark I'll follow ev'ry step he takes,   A notte folta io la sua traccio vigilio,
I'll choose the place and moment, and then you strike,   E il varco e l'ora scruto, il resto a te
I will be near you. Good hunting! Good hunting! Sword at the   Sarò tua scorta. A caccia! a caccia! Cingiti
Ready!   L'arco!

RODERIGO

Ah! I have sold my soul to you.   Sì! t'ho venduto onore a fe'.

IAGO

(Caught! I have caught you! Your feeble brain will serve me   (Corri al miraggio! il fragile tuo senno
Your feeble brain will serve me well,   Ha già confuso un sogno menzogner.
Foolish deluded man, deluded lover,   Segui l'astuto ed agile mio cenno,
Foolish deluded man, I'll soon achieve my goal.)   Amante illuso, io seguo il mio pensier.)

RODERIGO

(My fate is decided! The die is cast,   (Il dado è tratto! Impavido t'attendo,
Love drives me onward and I await my fate.   Ultima sorte, occulto mio destin.
Love is my guide but I fear some evil   Mi sprona amor, ma un avido, tremendo
Star of misfortune may lead me to harm.)   astro di morte infesta il mio cammin.)

OTELLO
(*rising and facing the crowd, with a terrifying expression*)

Now leave me!   Fuggite!

ALL

Ha!   Ciel!

OTELLO
(hurling himself at the crowd)

All men must flee Otello!   Tutti fuggite Otello!

(Off-stage fanfare.)

IAGO
(to the onlookers)

An old disease assails him,   Lo assale una malia
Depriving him of reason.   Che d'ogni senso il priva.

OTELLO
(in a ringing voice)

Who dares remain with me I brand as rebel.   Chi non si scosta è contro me rubello.

LODOVICO
(He tries to pull Desdemona away.)

Now leave him...   Mi segui...

VOICES
(from outside)

Evviva!   Evviva!

DESDEMONA
(freeing herself from Lodovico and running towards Otello)

My husband!   Mio sposo!

OTELLO
(in a terrifying voice, to Desdemona)

Wife of my bosom,   Anima mia,
My curse upon you!   Ti maledico!

ALL

Oh God!   Orror!

Exeunt all horrified, Desdemona with the aid of Emilia and Lodovico. **Scene Nine.** *Otello and Iago, alone.*

OTELLO
(growing more and more agitated)

But who can flee himself! Blood! Ah! Too   Fuggirmi io sol non so!...Sangue! Ah!
   dreadful   l'abbietto
To think of!... "How distressing!"   Pensiero!...ciò m'accora!

(He is unable to control himself.)

I see them both embracing... she gives my   Vederli insieme avvinti... il fazzoletto!...
   kerchief!...
Ah!   Ah!

(He faints.)

IAGO

(My poison works upon him.)   (Il mio velen lavora.)

FANFARE AND VOICES
(from outside)

Viva Otello!   Viva Otello!

IAGO
(listening to the shouts, then looking at Otello prostrate and senseless on the ground)

Still they're shouting his praises   L'eco della vittoria
Soon it will all be over.   Porge sua laude estrema.

(after a pause)

If on that brow I place my heel, what power   Chi può vietar che questa fronte io prema
On earth can stop me?   Col mio tallone?

FANFARE AND VOICES
(off-stage, growing louder)

Evviva Otello! Hail to   Evviva Otello! Gloria
The Lion of San Marco!   Al Leon di Venezia!

IAGO
(standing, with a gesture of gloating triumph, pointing to Otello, inert on the ground)

There lies your Lion!   Ecco il Leone!...

Curtain.

The text of the alternative Paris finale may be found on page 76.

Act Four

Desdemona's bedroom. Bed, prie-dieu, table, mirror, chairs. A hanging lamp burns before the image of the Madonna, which rests above the prie-dieu. A door on the right. It is night. A light burning on the table. [25] **Scene One.** *Desdemona and Emilia.*

EMILIA

Did he seem calmer?　　　　　　　　　　　Era più calmo?

DESDEMONA

　　　Yes, I think so. He bade me　　　　　　　　　Mi parea. M'ingiunse
Go to my chamber and await him there.　　Di coricarmi e d'attenderlo. Emilia,
　Emilia,
Let me ask you to lay upon my bed these　Te ne prego, distendi sul mio letto
Bridal sheets that were spread there on my　La mia candida veste nuzîale.
　wedding night.

(Emilia does so.)

Hear me. If I should chance to die before　Senti. Se pria di te morir dovessi,
　you.
See that I'm shrouded in one of these bridal　Mi seppellisci con un di quei veli.
　sheets.

EMILIA

But why this talk of dying?　　　　　　　Scacciate queste idee.

DESDEMONA

(sitting down without thinking before the mirror)
　　　I'm so unhappy. [26]　　　　　　　　　　　Son mesta tanto.
My mother once had a poor little maiden,　Mia madre aveva une povera ancella
As fair as she was faithful,　　　　　　Innamorata e bella;
And her name was　　　　　　　　　　　Era il suo nome
Barbara; she was　　　　　　　　　　　Barbara. Amava
In love and he she loved proved mad; she　Un uom che poi l'abbandonò; cantava
Had a song of willow, and she died singing　Una canzone: "La canzon del Salice".
　it.

(to Emilia)

Will you loosen my tresses.　　　　　　Mi disciogli le chiome:
And oh, this evening, how that unhappy　Io questa sera ho la memoria piena
　strain
Haunts my mind and will not leave me.　Di quella cantilena:
"The poor soul sat sighing　　　　[27]　"Piangea cantando
Beneath a willow,　　　　　　　　　　Nell'erma landa,
Beside a sad stream.　　　　　　　　　Piangea la mesta.
O willow! Willow! Willow!　　　　　　O Salce! Salce! Salce!
Alone and crying　　　　　　　　　　Sedea chinando
And lost in sad dream.　　　　　　　Sul sen la testa.
O willow! Willow! Willow!　　　　　　O Salce! Salce! Salce!
Sing Willow! This willow wreath I'll twine　Cantiamo! il Salce funebre
To be my bridal garland."　　　　　　Sarà la mia ghirlanda."
But hurry now; for soon will come Otello.　Affrettati; fra poco giunge Otello.
"The quiet stream ran by her where the　"Scorreano i rivi fra le zolle in fior,
　rushes grow,
In vain it tried to cheer her,　　　　Gemea quel core affranto,
And from her eyelids bitter tears would flow,　E dalle ciglia le sgorgava il cor
That stream grew mournful to hear her.　L'amara onda del pianto.
O willow! Willow! Willow!　　　　　　O Salce! Salce! Salce!
Sing willow! This willow wreath I'll twine　Cantiamo! il Salce funebre
To be my bridal garland."　　　　　　Sarà la mia ghirlanda."
"From branches high above sweet birds　"Scendean gli augelli a vol dai rami cupi
　came flying,
Moved by her tender moaning.　　　　Verso quel dolce canto,
And when they heard her piteous　　　E gli occhi suoi piangevan tanto, tanto
　lamentation,
The very stones were groaning."　　　Da impietosir le rupi."
And put away this necklace.　　　　　Riponi quest'anello.
Unhappy Barbara! Her plaintive story　Povera Barbara! Solea la storia
Always would end with a simple refrain!　Con questo semplice suono finir:
"Oh he was destined for deeds of glory,　"Egli era nato—per la sua gloria,
And I to love…"　　　　　　　　　　Io per amar…"

(breaking off)

70

But listen. Someone is coming. | Ascolta. Odo un lamento.
Quiet. Who's knocking at the door?… | Taci. Chi batte a quella porta?…

EMILIA

The wind. | È il vento.

DESDEMONA

"And I to love him and to die. Sing willow! | "Io per amarlo e per morir. Cantiamo!
O willow! Willow! Willow! | Salce! Salce! Salce!"
Farewell, Emilia. How my eyes are burning! | Emilia addio. Come m'ardon le ciglia!
It's a sure sign of weeping. Good night. | È presagio di pianto. Buona notte.
Ah! Emilia, Emilia, farewell. Emilia, | Ah, Emilia, Emilia, addio, Emilia, addio!
farewell.

Emilia turns to leave, then returns and Desdemona embraces her. Exit Emilia. **Scene Two.**
Desdemona alone. [25]

DESDEMONA
(*She goes to the prie-dieu.*)

Ave Maria, Mother of mercy, O loving | Ave Maria, piena di grazia, eletta
Holy Virgin, blessed be thy name; | Fra le spose e le vergini sei tu;
And blessed be the fruit, O gentle mother, | Sia benedetto il frutto, o benedetta,
Of thy most sacred womb, Jesu. | Di tue materne viscere, Gesù.
Pray for those who humbly kneel before [28] thee, | Prega per chi adorando a te si prostra,
Pray for those who sin, and for the sinless, | Prega pel peccator, per l'innocente
Pray for all who know oppression, and for the oppressor, | E pel debole oppresso e pel possente,
He too is wretched, and he needs thy pardon. | Misero anch'esso, tua pietà dimostra.
Pray for a maiden whose heart must bear | Prega per chi sotto l'oltraggio piega
Cruel grief, who suffers from unjust suspicion; | La fronte e sotto la malvagia sorte;
As we implore thee, pray for us | Per noi tu prega
Ever while we are living, in the hour of dying. | Sempre e nell'ora della nostra morte.

(*She remains kneeling, her forehead resting on the prie-dieu as if in silent prayer. Only the first and last words of the prayer can be heard.*)

Ave Maria . . . . | Ave Maria . . . .
. . . . | . . . .
. . . . In the hour of our dying. | . . . . nell'ora della morte.
Amen. | Amen.

She rises and goes to lie down. **Scene Three.** *Desdemona and Otello. Otello enters by a secret door, places a scimitar on the table, and pauses before the light, undecided whether to extinguish it. He looks at Desdemona. He puts out the light. The scene is illuminated only by the light from the prie-dieu. Otello, driven by a sudden burst of fury, approaches the bed; there he pauses.* [29,3c] *He gazes at Desdemona who is sleeping. He kisses her three times. At the third kiss, Desdemona awakens.* [8]

DESDEMONA
…Who's there?… | …Chi è là?…
(*She raises herself.*)
Otello? | Otello?

OTELLO
Yes! Have you prayed | Sì! Diceste questa sera
Tonight, Desdemona? | Le vostre preci?

DESDEMONA
I prayed. | Orai.

OTELLO
If you remember | Se vi sovviene
Some mortal sin you've committed which still | Di qualche colpa commessa che attenda
Remains unconfessed, you must ask for God's pardon. | Grazia dal ciel, imploratela tosto.

71

DESDEMONA

But why?   Perché?

OTELLO

And quickly! I do not wish to kill   T'affretta. Uccidere non voglio
Your immortal soul.   L'anima tua.

DESDEMONA

You mean to kill me?   D'uccider parli?

OTELLO

Yes. [30]   Sì.

DESDEMONA

Then God have mercy on me.   Pietà di me, mio Dio.

OTELLO

Amen.   Amen.

DESDEMONA

Otello,   E abbiate
And you have mercy too.   Pietà voi pure.

OTELLO

Think of your offences.   Pensa ai tuoi peccati.

DESDEMONA

All my sin has been love.   Mio peccato è l'amor.

OTELLO

For that I kill you.   Perciò tu muori.

DESDEMONA

Because I love you, you kill me? ...   E perché t'amo m'uccidi? ...

OTELLO

You love Cassio.   Ami Cassio.

DESDEMONA

No! I swear I do not!!   No! sull'anima mia!!

OTELLO

Do you deny you   Quel fazzoletto
Gave my kerchief to Cassio?   Ch'io ti donai gli desti.

DESDEMONA

I did not!   Non è vero!

OTELLO

Yet in his hand I saw it.   Nella sua man lo vidi.

DESDEMONA

I am not guilty!   Io rea non sono!

OTELLO

Confess it!   Confessa!

DESDEMONA

Truly.   Giuro!

OTELLO

Do not tell a falsehood...   Bada allo spergiuro...
Ah now confess as you lie on your deathbed.   Pensa che sei sul tuo letto di morte.

DESDEMONA

But not to die.   Non per morir.

OTELLO

To die this instant.   Per morir tosto.

DESDEMONA

God help me!   Aita!
I don't love Cassio... go and ask him. He'll   Cassio non amo... ch'ei qui venga... ei
tell you.   parli.

OTELLO

He's mute for ever.   Muto è per sempre.

DESDEMONA

Heaven! Murdered?   Cielo! Morto?

OTELLO
(*coldly*)

Justly.   Morto.

DESDEMONA

Then I'm lost! You have wronged him!   Son perduta!... ei tradito!

OTELLO
(*forcefully*)

You dare to mourn him?   E pianger l'osi?

DESDEMONA

Otello...do not murder me...   Otello...non uccidermi...

OTELLO

In vain you   Tu invano
Beg for mercy.   Ti difendi.

DESDEMONA
(*in desperation*)

O God I want to live...   Ch'io viva ancor...

OTELLO

So die now,   Giù, cadi,
You vile harlot!   Prostituta!...

DESDEMONA

Be kind!   Pietà!

OTELLO

Die!   Muori!!

DESDEMONA

Oh let me   Ch'io viva
Live tomorrow...   Questa notte...

OTELLO

No.   No.

DESDEMONA

An hour...   Un ora.

OTELLO

No.   No.

DESDEMONA

Then a moment...   Un istante.

OTELLO

No.   No.

DESDEMONA

While I say an Ave.   Sol ch'io dica un'Ave.

OTELLO

Too late now!   È tardi! È tardi!...

(*He strangles her. A cry from Desdemona. A knocking at the door is heard. He gazes at the inert body of Desdemona.*)

Calm and cold as the tomb.   Calma come la tomba.

EMILIA
(*from outside, again beating on the door*)
Otello! Otello!   Aprite! Aprite!

OTELLO
(*stumbling*)

Who's there! Who's knocking?   Chi è là! Chi batte?

EMILIA
(*as above*)

O my lord...   Signor mio...ven prego,
Come quickly, there's news that I must   Lasciate ch'io vi parli...Aprite!
  bring you!

OTELLO
(*opening*)

Emilia,   Emilia,
What's happened?   Che avvenne?

EMILIA
(*entering*)

There's been a murder! Cassio's killed   Un gran delitto! Cassio uccise
Roderigo.   Roderigo.

OTELLO

And Cassio?   E Cassio?

EMILIA

Lives.   Vive.

OTELLO

Cassio lives then!   Cassio vive!!

DESDEMONA
(from the bed)

I'm killed unjustly...I have been killed   Ingiustamente...uccisa ingiustamente...
unjustly...

EMILIA
(running to the bed)

What is that cry? Oh God!   Che geme là...Orror!

DESDEMONA

I am not guilty...   Muoio innocente...

EMILIA

O no! Whose hand was this?   Gran Dio!...Chi fu?

DESDEMONA

Ah no one...my own hand...And tell   Nessuno...io stessa...al mio...
My lord I never wronged him...Emilia...   Signor mi raccomanda...Emilia...
Farewell...   Addio...

(She dies.)

OTELLO

Oh she's a liar! I have killed her.   O mentitrice! io l'uccisi.

EMILIA

Cruel murderer!   Assassino!

OTELLO

She was Cassio's mistress. Just ask Iago.   Fu di Cassio la druda. A Jago il chiedi.

EMILIA

Ask Iago?   A Jago?

OTELLO

Yes, Iago.   A Jago.

EMILIA

Madman! And you believed him?   Stolto!! e tu il credesti?

OTELLO

You dare deny it?   Megarlo ardisci?!

(He springs towards Emilia.)

EMILIA

I don't fear you.   Non ti temo.

OTELLO
(He seizes hold of her.)

Silence!   Bada!

EMILIA
(She frees herself and runs towards the door, crying out at the top of her voice.)

Come here! Come help me! Come help me!   Olà! Soccorso! Aiuto! Otello uccise
Otello's murdered Desdemona.   Desdemona!

Scene Four. Otello, Emilia, Lodovico, Cassio, Iago, then Montano with armed attendants.

ALL
(except Otello and Emilia)

Who's shouting! O God! Ah no!   Quai grida! Orrore! Orrore!

EMILIA
(to Iago)

Iago, reveal all the truth to this madman.   Jago, smentisci quel vile assassino.
Did you believe that Desdemona betrayed   Hai tu creduto Desdemona infida?
him?
Answer!   Parla!

IAGO

So I believed.   Tal la credea.

74

OTELLO

That lovely kerchief
That once I gave her, to Cassio she freely gave it.

Quel fazzoletto
Che un di le diedi, a Cassio essa donava.

EMILIA

O you powers defend us!

O potenza divina!

IAGO
(*to Emilia*)

Quiet.

Taci.

EMILIA

No.
All shall be told!

No.
Tutto rivelo!

IAGO

Silence.

Taci.

EMILIA

No! that handkerchief
Was taken from my hand, was seized from
Me by Iago.

No! Costui
Dalla mia man quel fazzoletto svelse
A viva forza.

CASSIO

That handkerchief I found in
My room today.

E nella mia dimora
Trovai quel vel.

MONTANO
(*entering and pointing at Iago*)

Roderigo confessed it
As he died, he revealed all Iago's plotting.

Roderigo morente
Mi svelò di quest'uom l'arti nefande.

OTELLO
(*to Iago*)

Ah! Deny the charge!

Ah! discolpati!!

IAGO
(*fleeing*)

No.

No.

LODOVICO

Stop him!

Ferma.

MONTANO

Pursue him.

S'insegua.

(*Exit some, in pursuit of Iago*)

ALL

Set a guard on him!

Afferratelo!

OTELLO
(*lunging for his sword*)

O heav'n, have you no lightning left?!

E il ciel non ha più fulmini?!...

LODOVICO

Your sword to me!

La spada a me!

OTELLO

You dare it?! Do not fear me, [31]
Tho' I still have my sword here. Life's weary journey
Has reached its end. Oh! Glory! Otello's done.

Tant'osi!? Niun mi tema
S'anco armato mi vede. Ecco la fine
Del mio cammin... Oh! Gloria! Otello fu.

(*He lets fall the sword. He goes over to the bed and gazes upon Desdemona.*)

And you... how deathly pale you are! So weary, so silent, and lovely.
Ill-fated gentle creature born in a world of evil.
Cold now, cold as your pure tender virtue, and gone to heav'n now.
Desdemona! Desdemona! Ah! Dead! Dead! Dead now!

E tu... come sei pallida! e stanca, e muta, e bella.
Pia creatura nata sotto maligna stella.
Fredda come la casta tua vita, e in cielo assorta.
Desdemona! Desdemona!... Ah!... morta!... morta!... morta!...

(*stealthily taking a dagger from his clothes*)

I still am armed!

Ho un'arma ancor!

(*He stabs himself.*)

75

CASSIO

Ah! Stop him!   Ah! Ferma!

ALL

Oh Otello!   Sciagurato!

OTELLO

When I murdered you...wife...first I kissed you.	Pria d'ucciderti... sposa... ti baciai.
Now I'm dying...I lie in shades of darkness...	Or morendo... nell'ombra... ov'io mi giacio...
I'll kiss you...again I'll kiss you...once more I'll kiss you...	Un bacio...un bacio ancora...un altro bacio...

(*He dies.*)

Curtain.

The Paris Revision

Camille du Locle and Boito prepared a French translation of the libretto for the Paris première in 1894. Verdi took the opportunity to revise the concerted finale of the third act so that Iago's words could be clearly heard. (A ballet had, by Parisian convention, also to be added to the opera; Verdi inserted it after the entrance of the Venetian ambassadors.)

*

Iago explains his plan to Roderigo and obtains the reply 'My fate is in your hands', in both Italian and French versions. According to the French text, Iago then takes the centre of the stage and addresses the chorus.

IAGO
(in the centre of the stage)

All in this day of glory	Tous, en ce jour de gloire
Rejoice, put cares aside!	Chassons les noirs courroux!
See, our star is victorious,	L'astre de la Victoire
That star can be our guide.	Rayonne encor' sur nous.

(*The male chorus repeat these lines*)

WOMEN

Ah who can see her suff'ring!	Devant ce grand martyre
Tears fill my eyes with sorrow,	La charité soupire,
My heart is filled with grief.	Au fond de notre cœur,
All who behold her weep at the sight.	Devant le mal vainqueur.

The design by Nicola Benois for Act One of the Scala production which visited Covent Garden in 1950.
Below: his design for the last act of the Scala production. (Covent Garden Archives)

Discography In order of UK release. Available recordings only in stereo unless asterisked* and in Italian. Cassette tape numbers are also listed. A valuable review of all the performances on record by Alan Blyth is included in his *Opera on Record* (Hutchinson 1979).

Conductor Company/Chorus	Karajan VPO/Vienna State Opera Chorus	Serafin Rome Opera	Karajan Berlin Opera	Solti VPO/Vienna Boys Choir	Levine NPO/Ambrosian Opera Chorus	Barbirolli New Philharmonia
Otello	M. del Monaco	J. Vickers	J. Vickers	C. Cossutta	P. Domingo	J. McCracken
Iago	A. Protti	T. Gobbi	P. Glossop	G. Bacquier	S. Milnes	D. Fischer-Dieskau
Cassio	N. Romanato	F. Andreolli	A. Bottion	P. Dvorsky	F. Little	P. De Palma
Roderigo	A. Cesarini	M. Carlin	M. Senechal	K. Equiluz	P. Crook	–
Lodovico	F. Corena	F. Mazzoli	J. van Dam	K. Moll	P. Plishka	–
Montano	T. Krause	F. Calabrese	M. Machi	S. Dean	M. King	–
Desdemona	R. Tebaldi	L. Rysanek	M. Freni	M. Price	R. Scotto	G. Jones
Emilia	A.R. Satre	M. Parazzini	S. Malagu	J. Berbié	J. Kraft	–
Disc UK number	D55 D3	SER 5646–8	SLS 975	D102 D3	RLO 2951	
Tape UK number	K55 K32	RK 40001	TC-SLS 975	K102 K32	–	–
Excerpts (Disc) (US only) 25701					–	–
Excerpts (Tape)					–	–
Disc US number	1324	AGL3–1969	SX 3809	13130	CRL3–2951	S-3742
Disc US number	5-1324			–	CRK3-2951	4X3S-3742

Excerpts

Number	Artists	Disc Number	Tape Number
Highlights	Scotti/Tamagno/Melba	SAGA 7015	
Highlights	Santa Cecilia/Franci	SXL 6139	
Highlights	Covent Garden/Gardelli	TWO 390	
Highlights	La Scala/Abbado		3300 495
Brindisi/Credo	S. Milnes	SXL 6609	
Roderigo, beviam	T. Gobbi / J. Lanigan / J. Dobson /Solti	SET 392–3	
Già nella notte	L. Price/P. Domingo	ARLI 0840	
Già nella notte	J. Sutherland/L. Pavarotti	SXL 6828	KSXC 6828
Credo	G. Evans	SXL 6262	
Credo	R. Merrill	SXL 6083	
Fuggi O monstruosa colpa etc.	J. Bjorling/R. Merrill	RL 43243*	RK 43243*
Dio mi potevi/Niu mi tema	J. Vickers	LSB 4106	
Dio mi potevi/Niu mi tema	C. Bergonzi	D65 D3	
Ballet	Berlin PO/Karajan	2530 200	
Ballet	Berlin PO/Karajan		3300 206
Ballet	LSO/Almeida	6747 093	
Ballet	Cleveland/Maazel	SXL 6726	KSXC 6726
Era piu calma?	E. Schwarzkopf/M. Elkins	SXDW 3049	TC–SXDW 3049
Era piu calma?/Willow song	J. Sutherland	SXL 2257	
Willow song/Ave Maria	J. Sutherland	D65 D3	
Willow song/Ave Maria	R. Crespin	SDD 313	
Willow song/Ave Maria	E. Suliotis	SXL 6306	
Willow song/Ave Maria	M. Chiara	SXL 6605	
Era piu calma? etc.	R. Tebaldi	SDD 481	KSDC 481
Era piu calma?	L. Price	DPS 2001	

Bibliography

The chapter devoted to *Otello* in volume 3 of Julian Budden's *The Operas of Verdi* (Cassell, 1981) is the most distinguished study of the opera available in English. Fritz Noske's *The Signifier and the Signified* (The Hague, Nijhoff, 1977) is a notable collection of essays on Mozart and Verdi. Vincent Godefroy's *The Dramatic Genius of Verdi* (vol. 2, Gollancz, 1977) and *A Verdi Companion* (Gollancz, 1980) edited by William Weaver and Martin Chusid, contain stimulating chapters on this opera.

There are classic biographies by Francis Toye *Giuseppe Verdi, His Life and Works* (Heinemann, 1931) and Frank Walker *The Man Verdi* (Dent, 1962) in which many points have, however, been superseded by modern research.

Charles Osborne's edition of *The Letters of Giuseppe Verdi* (Gollancz, 1971) is the only English translation. *The Letters*, together with William Weaver's *Verdi: A Documentary Study* (Thames and Hudson, 1977) give many fascinating insights into Verdi's career. Pierre Petit's study of the man and his work (*Verdi*, Calder, 1962) is translated by Patrick Bowles in the Calderbook series.

Joseph Wechsberg's *Verdi* (Weidenfeld & Nicolson, 1974), Paul Hume's *Verdi, The Man and his Music* (Hutchinson, 1978) and Charles Osborne's *Verdi* (Macmillan, 1978) also contain many superb illustrations.